Learning
for
Real

Learning for Real

Teaching Content and Literacy

Across the Curriculum

Heidi Mills

Foreword by Lucy Calkins

HEINEMANN
Portsmouth, NH

Heinemann
361 Hanover Street
Portsmouth, NH 03801–3912
www.heinemann.com

Offices and agents throughout the world

All ideas and findings in this book represent the perspective of the author and do not necessarily represent the position of Richland School District Two or the University of South Carolina.

The Center for Inquiry K–5 magnet program of Richland School District Two and the University of South Carolina small-school partnership are not affiliated with the Center for Inquiry, Inc.

Heidi Mills wishes to thank the John C. Hungerpiller Professorship, University of South Carolina, for supporting her work as Curriculum, Research, and Development Specialist at the Center for Inquiry.

Library of Congress Cataloging-in-Publication Data
Mills, Heidi.
    Learning for real : teaching content and literacy across the curriculum / Heidi Mills ; foreword by Lucy Calkins.
        pages cm
    Includes bibliographical references.
    ISBN 978-0-325-04603-7
    1. Content area reading. 2. Inquiry-based learning. I. Calkins, Lucy II. Title.

    LB1050.455.M568 2014
    372.4—dc23   2013048642

Editor: Margaret LaRaia
Production: Victoria Merecki
Cover and interior designs: Suzanne Heiser
Typesetter: Gina Poirier, Gina Poirier Design
Video production: Melissa Cooperman
Manufacturing: Steve Bernier

Printed in the United States of America on acid-free paper
Sheridan 2020

For my dear friends and colleagues at

The Center for Inquiry in Columbia, South Carolina

Greenwood School of Inquiry in Hodges, South Carolina

Zaharis Elementary in Mesa, Arizona

Innovations Charter School in Kailua-Kona, Hawaii
> *and*

J. D. Parker Elementary in Stuart, Florida.

Thank you for illuminating what is possible for teachers and learners.

Contents

Chapter 1   A Cross-Content Area Vision of Balanced Literacy

Processes of Inquiry

Online Teaching Resources

Video Clip 6: *Inquiry into Rocks and Soil, Grade 1*

Video Clip 7: *Magazine Inquiry, Grade 5*

Video Clip 8: *Rosa Parks and Civil Rights, Grade 3*

Unit 5: *Rocks and Soil, Grade 1*

Unit 6: *Magazines, Grades 4 and 5*

Unit 7: *Civil and Human Rights, Grade 3*

All of the online teaching resources mentioned throughout this book can be found at www.heinemann.com/products/E04603.aspx (click on the Companion Resources tab).

Foreword

It was the videotapes of instruction at the Center for Inquiry (CFI) that first drew me in. I was floored by the vibrancy and rigor I saw on the clips that Heidi and Tim O'Keefe showed us during their keynote for the Day of Early Childhood at a National Council of Teachers of English (NCTE) conference. I—and the rest of the audience—urgently wanted to learn more. The teaching resembled reading and writing workshop instruction at its best, yet it also had a new depth and dimension. Perhaps part of what made me teary, watching those tapes, was the flood of nostalgia I felt for the olden days when teachers and children sang Pete Seeger songs lustily, and when lop-eared rabbits hopped about our classrooms. But much more than this, the videos of Tim's second- and third-grade classrooms and their discussion of them allowed me to see the power of truly taking the principles of reading and writing instruction across the curriculum. They showed me social studies, math, and science being taught in ways that gave students agency, that valued dialogue and inquiry, and that extended all that students learned from strong reading and writing workshops. To me, those video clips represented a next step for my entire organization.

Whereas typically the Teachers College Reading and Writing Project sends its staff to a national conference each year, that year fifteen of us flew to the tiny airport in Columbia, South Carolina, to spend a day learning from Heidi and the faculty at the Center for Inquiry. I count that one day as one of my most powerful days of learning ever.

As Heidi and I spoke later that evening, after a full day of visiting in half a dozen classrooms, I said to Heidi, "You owe it to the world to publish your work, through your videos and a book to go with them, so that others can see what my colleagues and I saw today." Little did I know that within a few years the Common Core State Standards (CCSS) would make it even more urgent that teachers across the nation learn from Heidi and her colleagues. She offers us a model for teaching and learning that allows children to achieve the rigor of the CCSS and to experience the joy that inspires them to learn more and work harder.

Exactly one year ago, I got a phone call. Heidi had discovered that she had a dangerous illness. It wasn't clear if she'd be okay. It seemed to me the state of South Carolina and the literacy leaders of the nation held our collective breath. We each did all we could do, sending her our prayers, our meditations, our best vibes, our most fervent hopes. I do not know what the prayers of others were, but mine included the prayer that she would have the chance to bring the beauty and power of her teaching to the whole world so that hundreds and thousands of children could learn in classrooms like those that my colleagues and I saw in her tapes and in her life when we visited CFI.

Heidi got better. And now, *hallelujah!* You have the opportunity to make the same journey that we made. You'll draw your chair alongside second graders as they work together to reconstruct a bat skeleton, their actions informed by posing questions, hypothesizing about bat physiology, and consulting print resources. You'll see first graders sharing observations and questions about the moon, and you'll see kindergartners living as ornithologists. You'll see first graders inquiring into rocks and soil, third graders composing a song about civil rights, and fifth graders creating their own magazines. Heidi shows us that when students' ideas are taken seriously, when their potential is not limited by our imagination but instead is supported through exploration and learning the skillfulness of inquiry, they can do work that is better than anything we could assign to them. This book and video brim with student work and student voices. By pulling your chair close and leaning in, you'll learn next-step ways to help students grow into the mathematicians, historians, readers, writers, inventors, and scientists that we need, and that they want to be.

If you're anything like my colleagues and me, this journey will change you; it will change you because it will allow you to live your ideals. You will see how focused inquiry is not overwhelming or chaotic, and how it can be used to create units that exceed the standards when framed as invitations for children to be engaged, curious, responsible, reflective people. You'll return to your own classroom filled with resolve to take all that you know about powerful reading and writing instruction and do even more than the Common Core State Standards ask you to do—only you'll do this work not because of a mandate, but because of love. Love of teaching, of kids, of each other, of reading and writing and inquiry. Love of the world.

—Lucy Calkins

Acknowledgments

As I reminisce about life and learning at the Center for Inquiry (CFI) over the past eighteen years, I'm filled with tremendous gratitude. There are so many who have shaped and been shaped by the world we've co-constructed over time. Although "Everyone and everything matters at the Center for Inquiry," as Steve Hefner, our previous superintendent noted, I must begin with our fearless leaders, Lyn Mueller and Amy Donnelly.

I am beyond grateful for the chance to coauthor our school culture in concert with Lyn and our remarkable teachers. For fifteen years we've envisioned, smiled, laughed, and cried together. We've posed and solved problems together. In Lyn's words, "We've dreamed and schemed together." Lyn has been steadfast through thick and thin. I most appreciate the fact that Lyn has made it possible for me to lead weekly curricular conversations with our faculty. We have created a culture of inquiry by growing beliefs and practices individually and collectively through weekly curricular conversations. Lyn makes sure classes are covered for lunch and beyond on Thursdays to build ongoing professional development into the fabric of the school day. Thank you, thank you, thank you.

Before Lyn, there was Amy Donnelly. It was Amy who worked in concert with the founding faculty and district administrators in Richland School District Two to envision, launch, and sustain our school for the first three, most challenging, years. Amy's impact is still felt today. She set the standard for joyful rigor. Amy institutionalized a number of whole school rituals such as student-led conferences, Monday morning and Friday afternoon whole-school gatherings, and our exquisite fifth-grade graduation ceremony. Amy gave three years of her life to CFI and those of us who have had the privilege of living and learning together since then have her to thank for bringing us into being.

Beyond a doubt, my CFI teaching colleagues have become the most trusted and valued mentors of my career. When I reflect on our school's history, the period when Dori Gilbert, Jennifer Barnes, Tim O'Keefe, Susanne Pender, Brent Petersen, Julie Waugh, and Brenna Osborne lived and learned together were "our wonder years." When this collection of hearts and minds came together, everything came together. Their legacy lives on through the beliefs and practices that permeate our school culture today. They established the fertile ground for our current faculty to grow and change individually and collectively. I'm grateful to our newest faculty members, Susan Bolte, Michelle Kimpson, Melissa Klosterman, Chris Hass, Brandon Foote, Tameka Breland, Tammy Vice, Scott Johnson, and Amanda Mahowald, for sowing fresh seeds. They are reinvigorating life at CFI by bringing foundational beliefs and practices to life in their own ways. They are honoring our past while building a promising future. Their unique, brilliant contributions permeate this book and our school culture. It also brings me tremendous satisfaction to welcome Emily Whitecotton to our world. Although this is her first year on the faculty, it feels like she has always been with us. Her transition has been seamless.

Jaretta Belcher and Lisa Smith offered invaluable support as kindergarten assistants. When visiting the kindergarten classrooms, it's often hard to distinguish the teachers from the assistants because Jaretta and Lisa engage in careful kidwatching as they support learning and learners alongside their teaching colleagues. Susie King, Melanie Bardin, Danielle Hucks, and Rachel Slotkis are equally remarkable as they lead from behind as teaching assistants. Their kindness, focused attention, and commitment to their children's academic success are unparalleled. A special thank you to Becky Watkins for helping our students learn how to look and act on the world as artists. Last, but certainly not least, I want to thank Angie Debeaugrine from the bottom of my heart. Angie is so much more than the school secretary. She truly holds everyone and everything together. I can't imagine how we would function without her open heart, sharp mind, and strategic actions.

After working with CFI and other schools across the country, I've learned the crucial role district office personnel play in making or breaking school innovations. I honestly believe we are thriving because Steve Hefner and Debbie Hamm, our former and current superintendents, have offered big picture wisdom and unwavering support from their positions of power. District office leadership and support from the Richland School District Two school board have made it possible for us to succeed over the years. Thank you.

Over the past three years I have had the privilege of collaborating with the Greenwood School of Inquiry (GSI) in Hodges, South Carolina. When I launched my work with the faculty I had the same feeling I had when we were expecting our second child. I couldn't imagine loving anyone as much as Devin. Then Colin came along and I learned our hearts simply grow larger. So too with my colleagues at GSI . . . I have fallen in love with my new colleagues and am grateful for the chance to share in their professional journey. Thank you to the school and district leadership teams Cathy Chalmers, Pearly Milton, Pat Ross, Darrell Johnson, Roger Richburg, Frances Gilliam, Linda Hill, and Claudia Jennings for envisioning new possibilities for the teachers and students at Hodges Elementary. Thank you to my dear teaching colleagues Elizabeth Arnold, Lauren Alverson, Debbie Babb, Katie Babb, Jennifer Baker, Gail Behrendt, Dianne Calvert, Juanita Davis, Emmy Evans, Lori Lloyd, Claudia McCier, Susan Nickles, Renee Ott, Tara Ramsey, Stephanie Rudman, Sally Strawhorne, Claire Thompson, and Kristi Wiles. I truly appreciate your vision, commitment, inspiration and perseverance. I also want to thank Miss Janice for making the school sparkle while making sure that all hearts and minds that live and learn there have the opportunity to shine.

As I envisioned and wrote each chapter in this book, I held principals Mike Oliver, Jennifer Hiro, Mary McWilliams White, and their school faculties in the front of my mind. Their schools were my primary audience as I composed and revised. Their connections and questions over the years helped me better understand how to help others transfer and transform insights from CFI to diverse school settings across the country. I treasure the memories and lessons learned from my work with Zaharis Elementary, Innovations Public Charter School, and J.D. Parker Elementary. Thank you for making a profound difference in my personal and professional life.

Although there are many from within Richland School District Two who helped make us who we are today, I can honestly say it's the unprecedented support from my administrators and colleagues at the University of South Carolina who have made it possible for our partnership to work so fluidly. I must begin by thanking Susi Long, my secular angel, for being such a thoughtful, caring, devoted, and insightful friend and colleague. Susi's appreciation of CFI and her commitment to social justice always make me mindful of the critical work and responsibility we have ahead of us. I am grateful for the time Louise Jennings spent living and learning alongside us at CFI as our school ethnographer. She helped us carefully capture and document processes that underpin a discourse of inquiry by following one cohort of students from kindergarten through graduation in our early years. From the moment I picked Tasha Laman up at the airport for her interview at USC, she has brought goodness and light to our world. She demonstrates her appreciation of CFI by regularly accessing us as a demonstration site for her undergraduate students. I am especially appreciative of the ways Diane Stephens has nurtured my work at CFI over the years. She, more than anyone in a position of power at USC, honored my work and life by recommending that my work at CFI count as part of my load. I am also appreciative of Gloria Boutte, Diane DeFord, Harvey Allen, Les Sternberg, Mike Seaman, Michelle Crisp, and Lemuel Watson for their unwavering commitment. They value and recognize my efforts to unite teaching, scholarship, and service through my work at the Center for Inquiry. Each, in their own ways, enhances the impact of CFI through their own initiatives.

Then there are those who gave form to my thinking long ago. Although they are distant teachers now, Jerry Harste, Carolyn Burke, Jean Anne Clyde, Kathryn Mitchell Pierce, David and Phyllis Whitin, and Kathy Short's theoretical fingerprints can be found throughout our school and across this book. I will always be grateful for the chance to think up with them as a doctoral student at Indiana University.

It's a challenge to find adequate words to express my heartfelt gratitude for the chance to work so closely with my editor, Margaret LaRaia. Margaret has had a profound influence on my writing, work, and life. I constantly find myself looking at our classrooms and the world through her soft, incredibly perceptive eyes. She has become a powerful presence in my life. I carry her spirit and insights with me now. She is an amazing writing coach who offers tremendous clarity about the nature of support teachers need and deserve. It was such a collaborative effort, I consider this "our" book. The design team at Heinemann complemented and extended the work Margaret and I did together. Victoria Merecki is a masterful production editor. She was responsive to my individual requests while maintaining a solid vision of the whole. Her meticulous attention to detail ensured the whole would be greater than the sum of its parts. I loved and learned from the editorial changes Alan Huisman suggested on the manuscript. He is one of Heinemann's many gifts. Thank you also to Heinemann's Design Manager, Suzanne Heiser, for her exquisite cover and text designs. And the gifts keep coming . . . I am beyond thrilled with Melissa Cooperman's skillful adaptations of the authentic classroom video footage I provided. She made brilliant editing decisions and masterfully transformed the footage. I commend Melissa for her technical prowess and her capacity to convey moments that count. I'm astounded by Heinemann Marketing Manager Eric Chalek's capacity to capture the essence of our work and this book so clearly and succinctly. Thank you, Eric.

Thank you to Katie Wood Ray for being one of our most devoted advocates and significant mentors over the years. Katie has made several trips to visit our school and consistently attends our presentations at NCTE. We can always count on Katie to see more in us than we see in ourselves. We can also count on her to push us to outgrow ourselves with compelling questions and thoughtful recommendations. Katie's presence in our lives, and in the profession at large, is a genuine present.

Thanks also to Lucy Calkins, who literally made it possible for me to finish this book. It takes my breath away when I think about Lucy's sphere of influence in the world in light of her willingness to intervene at just the right moment, in just the right way, when I faced an incredible health challenge last year. Lucy's role in my personal and professional life has been synchronistic across my career. She appreciated and nurtured my collaborative research with Tim O'Keefe long before we believed the

Center for Inquiry into being. For over twenty-five years, Lucy seemed to "see us" and challenge us simultaneously. I'm humbled and energized when in her presence. She helps me notice and name the value of our work while pushing me to recognize the urgency and complexity of enhancing our impact.

I am more than grateful for how everything evolved with my surgery last year. There were so many gifts embedded in the challenges. The love and prayers from my immediate family, Paula, Bill, Donna, and Guy Mills and their families with our boys, Devin and Colin, would have been enough to sustain me, I'm quite sure. Yet I had so much more. I was truly overwhelmed by the outpouring of love, prayers, gifts, and healing energy from friends, family, and colleagues across the country. Everyone and everything worked together to give me strength, hope, and comfort. You know who you are and I will forever treasure you. As Douglas Wood reminds us, "We don't give thanks because we are happy. We are happy because we give thanks." It brings me tremendous joy to thank you from the bottom of my heart.

One thing I know for sure is that my mother-in-law, Ruthanne Burns, would have been most proud of this work and of her son's role in it. She was always our greatest fan. We deeply miss her presence in our personal and professional lives.

Finally, I want to thank Tim O'Keefe for being the husband, friend, father, and teacher of my dreams. More than anyone, Tim has set the standard for teaching and teachers in my world. More than anyone, Tim has shaped the essence of CFI. I am in awe of, and humbled by, his wisdom, kindness, rigor, professionalism, honesty, his commitment to justice, and his no-nonsense attitude about life and learning. He inspires me as a mother, teacher, and learner. Tim is a gift to our family, our profession, and humanity. Thank you . . . THE BIG THANK YOU.

Introduction: Teaching as Inquiry

We all know how exhilarating it is to learn something new, to develop expertise around a passion, to share with a community, to learn alongside others who are deeply interested in the same topic, sport, or hobby. We've experienced this since we were very young, although we may not remember it. The natural wonder that propelled us through childhood is still deep inside us—and inside the children we teach. When we watch a child drop to the ground to observe a spider, dash to her room, grab a field guide, and then match the live specimen to a photograph, we remember what it means to inquire: to follow the logic of an authentic question.

Each time we encounter an anomaly or witness a spectacular natural phenomenon, we wonder about it. We gather information when adopting a baby or preparing to give birth ourselves. We investigate how to make wise choices when purchasing a car, helping the homeless, playing tennis or golf, learning to quilt, becoming a beekeeper, or taking up gardening. Whenever we advocate for a social, spiritual, or political cause (or just plan a vacation), we remember what authentic learning looks, sounds, and feels like.

What Is the Process of Inquiry?

When learning something new we seek to understand first by making careful observations and posing pertinent questions. We learn about the tools or resources of the discipline and how to use them. We talk with others. We seek out mentors. We develop the unique vocabulary used in the discipline, first to comprehend and then to share our thinking. We compare what we notice in life (*primary sources*) with information others have compiled (*secondary sources*). We reflect, read some more, and pose new questions. Then we gather additional information from direct observation, published research, and trusted personal sources—doctors, social workers, clergy members, coaches, travel agents, consumer advocates. When we truly care about a topic, we deliberately inquire. We embrace the process naturally as we amass critical information and learning strategies. When we are invested in our personal inquiries, we lead passionate, wide-awake lives.

Learning something new involves investigating how others—biologists, climatologists, anthropologists, historians, authors, and botanists—go about it. This is just what we can do as teachers to bring content and literacy learning to life in truly authentic ways. Kindergarten and first-grade teacher Susan Bolte recently sent me an email describing a unit of study she is writing for her young scientists:

> *I want to communicate to the kids just how exhilarating it is to be out in the field, doing the real and important work of scientists. I want them to experience the satisfaction of experiencing the world, wonder about the things they have experienced, and then create ways in which to answer their own questions.*

Hers is a vision so many teachers share but wonder how to bring to life.

Given today's complex demands of public school teaching—the codified standards and formal assessments—you may think this vision of teaching is too Pollyanna for the realities of your teaching life. I understand. But I've shared these stories, strategies, and video clips with teachers in very diverse settings across the United States and Canada. They have taken these beliefs and practices and made them their own, in their own ways. And in the process they have rediscovered the joy of teaching.

Teaching through inquiry doesn't mean more (or less) work. It means acknowledging that what we do every day in the classroom with our students is creative, strategic, and reflective. True teaching is learning. Our teaching practices model the processes of inquiry we want students to own and use for themselves. But this is more than just demonstration. Like all relationships, teaching is reciprocal. By viewing teaching as inquiry, we get back as much—maybe more—than we give. We allow ourselves to be surprised. We accept that we, and our students, don't know everything, but that we can get smarter together. We create learning experiences that give us, and our students, the space to grow.

When Susan Bolte invited me to join her first graders' journey through astronomy, I didn't expect to be changed by the experience. You'll find her unit online, and you'll read more about her teaching and see a video clip in Chapter 7, but first let's think about how we as adults can be changed by our teaching. For example, even though I earned an A in astronomy in college, Susan's first graders taught me how to see the moon with new eyes. I always appreciated the moon's natural beauty, but now on my nightly walks with my husband I pause with a sense of wonder at what I know about the moon and how it's connected to what I see. I am now more intentional, more contemplative as I live and learn. When I glance into the sky or notice the moon's reflection on the lake, I think of Susan and her first graders sharing their moon journal entries, of their connections and questions. Susan and her first graders brought astronomy to life in ways that mattered. We all learned a great deal—and we were changed by it.

We Don't Have to Know Everything

The emotion of joyful surprise at something unexpected—wonder—can only happen if we accept that we don't know everything. The capacity for wonder is innate in human beings. Whenever we learn something new, our brain experiences the same biochemical reaction of pleasure at discovery as the first person who made that discovery. Our brains are made to motivate us to learn more: when we learn something new, our brains release dopamine, which rewards us for our learning efforts and reinforces this learning behavior. If we understand what triggers the emotional response of curiosity, then perhaps we can dismiss the idea that teachers need to know everything and instead focus on how we can nurture our students' curiosity and our own.

We Give Ourselves Opportunities to Pay Attention

To foster curiosity, we have to give ourselves opportunities to pay attention, which are acts of willful selection: choosing one thing to observe while ignoring others. Think about our busy lives and the chaos that can be a school day: In the flurry of trying to do everything, we often never fully do anything. In Chapter 1, I explain some classroom structures and strategies that support the act of paying attention. However, it's also worthwhile to think about how we can give ourselves opportunities to pay attention. We don't need to restrict ourselves to school-related subjects. Although reading is an act of paying attention, it doesn't have to be the only one—people-watching on the bus, walking through your neighborhood, and trying to listen more and talk less are all acts of attention. Being mindful of where, and how fully, we direct our attention can make us better teachers.

We Question What We Know

Attention is observation. We identify what is familiar and what is unfamiliar, what is known and unknown. In Chapter 2, you'll learn how to scaffold students' observations through specific tools and strategies so they can identify and reflect on their observations. However, part of identifying what we already know means being open to the possibility that what we *think* we know might be wrong, or that we might not know something as fully as we could. This may sound like a philosophical riddle, but consider, for example, what it means to know a place. Knowledge of it develops over time and through a variety of experiences. We may think we understand a place—its culture and the people who live there—but, especially if we haven't been there before, we risk stereotyping or jumping to conclusions without first observing and questioning.

We Know and Let Ourselves Be Known by Our Students

What does this mean for us as teachers? The most important modeling we do is showing that we're curious about what children think, that we're open to being surprised and impressed by them. Fourth- and fifth-grade teacher Julie Waugh describes it as "unanxious expectation." We simply expect that children will say or do something thoughtful, brilliant, or helpful. When children know that we're interested in and care about the thinking they generate, they become more invested in taking the risks and doing the work required to develop their own thinking. What's more, when they realize that their thinking also informs and supports the work of the class as a whole, they feel an even greater sense of responsibility about their learning. We lay the groundwork through planning (Chapter 7), recurrent structures and practices (Chapter 8), and our stance as inquiring teachers, but the daily life of the classroom has the energy of true collaboration, just like any good conversation.

We set expectations for classroom inquiry to be joyful, meaningful work by:

- creating opportunities for our kids and us to teach and learn from everyone in the room,
- maintaining habits of reflection, both for our kids about their learning and for us about what and how our kids are learning, and
- asking our kids to use the information gathered through ongoing reflection to identify their strengths and needs as learners.

By doing these things, we know our kids better, our kids know their classmates and us better, and our kids know themselves as learners better (see Figure I.1, Mills 2005).

Knowing and Being Known

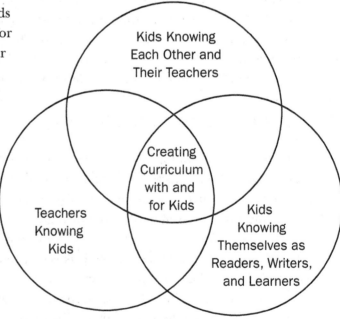

Kids Knowing Each Other and Their Teachers

Creating Curriculum with and for Kids

Teachers Knowing Kids

Kids Knowing Themselves as Readers, Writers, and Learners

Figure I.1

Our Approach to the Process of Inquiry

Each time we teach an inquiry unit we have a fresh experience—we do not simply walk our children through a set of predetermined activities. We bring our plans to life in concert with our students. This may sound pie-in-the-sky, but let's think about what this can look like in our classrooms. A simple shift in our thinking and planning can transform how we teach content and content literacy:

- Instead of teaching about plants, we invite children to think, work, and communicate as botanists.
- Instead of teaching about a culture, we help children pose questions and make observations as anthropologists.
- Instead of teaching about insects, we show children how to look at the world and use the tools of entomologists.
- Instead of teaching about history, we explore how historians use primary and secondary sources to reconstruct events and record stories of significant moments.

This shift in thinking reframes how Susan Bolte constructs her first-grade curriculum. Her curriculum does more than cover topics; it provides students with experiences that help them grow into strategic readers, writers, mathematicians, scientists, and social scientists. Susan and her K–5 colleagues devote as much time to teaching children *how* to learn as *what* to learn.

In this book, you'll learn how to plan for inquiry in a way that promotes literacy throughout the day and across the content areas. In the video clips, you'll see what that can look like in a variety of classrooms. A few years ago I asked two Center for Inquiry fifth graders what made their school special. One exclaimed, "It's cool to know things here!" The other answered, "Our school is a reading machine." They were describing a school culture in which literacy and content aren't separate but linked. This link is not idiosyncratic or ephemeral. It is based on the following universal processes of inquiry, which are relevant to small and tall learners, novices to experts, in all content areas and professions.

- Carefully observe the world using the tools and strategies of the discipline (Chapter 2).
- Pose questions and investigate/solve problems from numerous perspectives (Chapter 3).
- Access primary and secondary sources in complementary ways (Chapter 4).

- Use the language of inquiry and disciplines to learn and communicate new understanding (Chapter 5).
- Use reflection and self-evaluation to grow and change (Chapter 6).

As Carl Sandburg put it, "Nothing happens unless first a dream." In this book, lots of classroom-tested tools will help you realize what you dream for your students. These tools are not scripts, but structures and strategies that will give you what you need to be your best as a teacher and help your students reach their potential. After all, teachers need as much space as students do to grow and innovate. Here you'll find the support needed to build curriculum based on children's lives as well as fulfill the expectations of the Common Core standards or district/state expectations. Trying something different often means taking a risk, and there's plenty of evidence here to prove that doing so is worth it!

Chapter 1

A Cross-Content Area Vision of Balanced Literacy

Before we jump into the "how-to," let's first address some of the thinking that makes teachers resistant to inquiry, particularly at the primary grades. Some argue that reading instruction in grades K–2 should be focused solely on supporting children in learning to read and write so that later, in grades 3–5, children can focus on reading and writing to learn. This distinction is artificial, and I'll explain why.

Learning to Read While Reading to Learn

As soon as children are read to, they show awareness of both content and the way the content is delivered. They're reading to learn while they're learning how to read. They may not be able to name all of what they're experiencing in a text, but they're experiencing it; to pretend otherwise is to limit important learning opportunities for kids. Part of offering rich learning experiences for kids is exposing them to many different kinds of texts right away. I've seen how kindergartners can navigate, interpret, and compose nonfiction texts—if teachers provide the right support. At the Center for Inquiry (CFI), teachers give equal attention to strategies for reading and writing both nonfiction and fictional texts. Kindergartners learn nonfiction text features and structures alongside noticing and naming capital letters, punctuation, onset and rhyme patterns, story structure, alliteration, and so on. Young readers build their understanding of texts so that they learn when to use strategies; some strategies are helpful for any text and others are specific to the kind of text they're reading. When nonfiction texts are an integral part of classroom life, kindergartners and first graders select them as often as fourth and fifth graders do during independent reading. When, from the beginning of their literacy careers, students compose nonfiction texts during writing workshop and during integrated units of study, the value and understanding of nonfiction texts is reinforced and deepened.

When a child chooses a book on red-eyed tree frogs, for example, he's most likely choosing it because of his interest in the topic and/or the design of the book. He might also be choosing to read it because a teacher has structured independent reading time, because he's been told to pick from a collection of books on amphibians, or because he knows he can read that book without too much difficulty. All of these reasons for reading this particular book are interconnected. *Learning about* and *learning through* are ongoing—and inseparable—processes. Regardless of the standards or unit of study, reading is a vehicle for students to develop their understanding of the world.

If supported, students inquire during reading and writing workshops as much as they do during integrated units of study in the sciences or social sciences. Michael Halliday explains that children need opportunities to learn language, learn about language, and learn through language (1975). This is what we mean by "balanced literacy." Reading and writing workshops are curricular structures that give students lots of reading and writing time, and they are done in an authentic context. They learn by doing, just as children learn to talk by talking, and practice produces more accomplished, strategic, effective readers and writers. Not "independent practice" of a specific strategy or understanding, but self-directed use. We want students to have experiences that are discoveries for them. "What happens if . . . ?" Wondering and finding out is self-directed inquiry that drives real learning.

Reading and writing workshops provide space and time for students to investigate the ways writers can effectively construct and share meaning (well-crafted language, wondrous words, text structures and features). By establishing a connection to science and social studies through cross-content area units of study, students transfer what they've learned in meaningful ways; that is, they learn through reading and writing when inquiring in the sciences and social sciences.

As I work with teachers across the country, I've noticed that, as a profession, we have made tremendous progress in establishing solid reading and writing workshops. We understand that effective reading and writing workshops promote learning about language and learning through language (Mills, O'Keefe, and Jennings 2004; Short 1997). This book and the accompanying video clips extend that idea to content learning and content literacy. It's about thinking strategies that make a difference across content areas. For too long, literacy practices have been artificially constricted in schools. The United Nations Educational, Scientific and Cultural Organization (UNESCO) defines literacy as:

> *the ability to identify, understand, interpret, create, communicate and compute, using printed and written materials associated with varying contexts. Literacy involves a continuum of learning in enabling individuals to achieve their goals, to develop their knowledge and potential, and to participate fully in their community and wider society.*

We've done good work addressing the first sentence of the definition, but how consistently have we addressed the second sentence in our classrooms? Not enough yet, but we can.

Learning to Read and Write While Learning About: Kindergarten Ornithology Unit

By teaching children processes for learning, we help them learn how to learn. We are teaching them how to explore, understand, and communicate as readers, writers, mathematicians, scientists, and social scientists. This stance makes all the difference in the world: it makes them self-sufficient, or at least brings them closer to self-sufficiency.

The processes of inquiry aren't invisible. Walking into Dori Gilbert's kindergarten classroom (Figure 1.1), you see them at work. On display and in use are artifacts of students' experiences learning how to learn (processes and strategies) and what to learn (content). Take a virtual tour by studying the photographs. How and what are children learning about birds? After you've reflected, read my explanation.

Figure 1.1 Thinking, Talking, and Acting Like Ornithologists in Kindergarten

Carefully Observe the World Using Tools and Strategies of the Discipline

Because Dori wants her students to observe birds carefully using the tools and strategies of ornithologists, she creates a bird observatory in her classroom stocked with diverse bird nests and feathers, binoculars for bird watching, and magnifying lenses to examine the nests' and feathers' material and construction. This observatory isn't a classroom decoration; it's an active place for five and six year olds to work as ornithologists.

Ornithologists are intentional and systematic about documenting the birds they spot, and Dori's birders learn to do this well. Students document their bird-watching observations by completing a bar graph featuring birds sighted on the school grounds (Figure 1.2), or sketching and writing about live birds or artifacts such as feathers and nests in the class bird journal.

During science workshop, in small groups or as a class, they develop strategies for collecting and analyzing data about birds. Dori takes her students outside where they identify the birds they see, carefully coloring a box in the appropriate column of a graph they're carrying on a clipboard. After Dori is confident the children understand how to identify common birds found in South Carolina in the winter and how to graph quantitative data, for homework the children collect, analyze, and display information on the birds they see at home.

Use the Language of Inquiry to Learn and Communicate New Understanding

To help students not just understand but also use the language of ornithologists, Dori creates a "wondrous word wall," starting with words from her daily read-alouds and adding more as students share their learning. Dori keeps a packet of sticky notes and a pen next to her rocking chair. Before reading aloud she reminds her students to listen for interesting, beautiful, or puzzling words that ornithologists use. After she finishes, students share words they notice (*fledgling*, for example), and talk about and reflect on

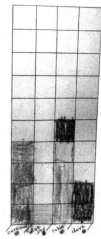

Data Collection
Which birds do we see at CFI

Figure 1.2

them. Then Dori writes these wondrous words on sentence strips, asks the children who

Figure 1.3

shared the words to illustrate them, and posts the wondrous words with illustrations on the wall (see Figure 1.3). The wondrous words wall is referred to regularly during writing workshop when children compose nonfiction texts about birds, allowing them to write many sophisticated scientific words conventionally. Their ownership of these words is one more aspect of their taking on the identity of ornithologists.

Pose and Investigate Questions from Numerous Perspectives

Dori encourages her ornithologists to pose questions as they observe nests, feathers, and bird behavior and as they read or listen to books about birds. Then she posts their questions (see Figure 1.4) and identifies patterns among them. She plans teaching demonstrations, designs learning engagements, and collects resources that help the students investigate their questions. She often launches a science workshop

Figure 1.4 Shared Question

demonstration with one or two "I wonder" questions, explicitly connecting the questions with the work students are doing together as ornithologists. She also chooses daily read-alouds that will answer these questions. Later, when several children ask questions about the speed and height of birds' flight, she invites them to read their questions to the class and asks students to listen for possible answers as she reads aloud a story that includes this information.

Strategically Access Primary and Secondary Sources in Complementary Ways

Dori has her students observe primary sources (live birds, feathers, nests) and pose questions about what they notice. Next she demonstrates turning to secondary sources, such as nonfiction books, magazines, and websites, to investigate or explore their questions. For example, Gail Gibbons' books—*Owls* (2006), *Penguins!* (1999), and *Chicks & Chickens* (2005)—each explain one species of bird, but by comparing and contrasting the characteristics of each species, students learn important shared and distinguishing characteristics.

When a number of students wondered how birds build nests and what materials they use, Dori taught them to use magnifying glasses (as scientists do) to analyze bird nests carefully. Students solidify and extend their observations by sketching and labeling nests (see Figure 1.5).

Figure 1.5
Pine Straw, Sticks, Cotton, Mud, Food, Leaves

Mud and Sticks and Feathers

Then Dori reads excerpts from several informational texts, particularly those with strong images (see Figure 1.6), to help students better understand how and why birds build nests from different materials in different locations.

Andersen, Hans Christian. *The Ugly Duckling.* New York: Knopf, 1986.
Anholt, Laurence. *The Magpie Song.* Boston: Houghton Mifflin, 1996.
Bunting, Eve. *Secret Place.* New York: Clarion Books, 1996.
Carlstrom, Nancy. *Goodbye, Geese.* New York: Philomel Books, 1991.
Deedy, Carmen Agra. *Agatha's Feather Bed: Not Just Another Wild Goose Story.* Atlanta: Peachtree Publishers, 1991.
Ehlert, Lois. *Feathers for Lunch.* San Diego: Harcourt Brace Jovanovich, 1990.
Fox, Mem. *Feathers and Fools.* San Diego: Harcourt Brace, 1996.
George, Jean Craighead. *Luck.* New York: Laura Geringer Books, 2006.
Gibbons, Gail. *Gulls, Gulls, Gulls.* New York: Holiday House, 1997.
Gibbons, Gail. *Owls.* New York: Holiday House, 2005.
Gibbons, Gail. *The Puffins Are Back.* New York: HarperCollins, 1991.
Gibbons, Gail. *Soaring With the Wind: The Bald Eagle.* New York: Morrow Junior Books, 1998.
Knowles, Sheena. *Edward the Emu.* New York: HarperTrophy, 1998.
Lewin, Betsy. *Booby Hatch.* New York: Clarion Books, 1995.
McMillan, Bruce. *The Days of the Ducklings.* Boston: Houghton Mifflin, 2001.
Peters, Lisa Westberg. *This Way Home.* New York: H. Holt, 1994.
Ring, Elizabeth. *Loon at Northwood Lake.* Norwalk, CT: Soundprints, 1997.
Rockwell, Norman. *Willie Was Different: A Children's Story.* Stockbridge, MA: Berkshire House Publishers, 1994.
Sierra, Judy. *Antarctic Antics: A Book of Penguin Poems.* San Diego: Harcourt Brace & Co., 1998.

Figure 1.6   *continues*

van Frankenhuyzen, Robbyn Smith. *Adopted by an Owl: The True Story of Jackson the Owl*. Chelsea, MI: Sleeping Bear Press, 2001.
Willis, Nancy Carol. *The Robins in Your Backyard*. Montchanin, DE: Cucumber Island Storytellers, 1996.
Wright, Lynn Floyd. *The Prison Bird*. Columbia, SC: Worry Wart, 1991.
Yashima, Taro. *Crow Boy*. New York: Viking Press, 1955.
Yolen, Jane. *Owl Moon*. New York: Philomel Books, 1987.
Science Kit
Echols, Jean. *Penguins and Their Young. Great Explorations in Math and Science* (GEMS). University of California at Berkeley: Lawrence Hall of Science, 1996.
Film
March of the Penguins. Warner Brothers Entertainment Inc., 2005.

Figure 1.6 continued

Texts were chosen not for coverage of topics on standards, but for their ability to synthesize and reflect experts' (in this case, ornithologists') understanding and curiosity. In this way, no one text becomes a single authority; instead, students learn to evaluate and synthesize understandings across primary and secondary sources.

Use Reflection and Self-Evaluation to Grow and Change

Scientists regularly reflect on their own learning as well as that of their colleagues, so Dori invites her students to have this same experience. Reflecting on content and processes deepens learning and gives children opportunities to teach and learn from one another.

Talk is an important tool for reflection. Because Dori knows that kindergartners' oral language often conveys their understanding better than their writing and drawing, she often documents the words and phrases students use when talking about birds. She pays careful attention to whether children are using words such as *herbivore, carnivore, omnivore, predator,* and *prey* correctly. She also records and reviews their "I wonder" questions, because she believes they should ask better questions at the end of an inquiry than at the start.

Charts document students' developing understanding and are assessed against the science standards about characteristics of organisms ("common features and needs of birds," in this case). The class chart shown in Figure 1.7 documents how living as ornithologists has changed these kindergartners and helped them grow.

The Gail Gibbons' books on birds (*Owls, Penguins!* and *Chicks & Chickens*) and other secondary sources read for information about birds also inform students' understanding of how information about birds can be communicated. As a culminating experience, Dori's students compose nonfiction books to showcase their expertise as young ornithologists as well as what they've learned about text features and text structures. They

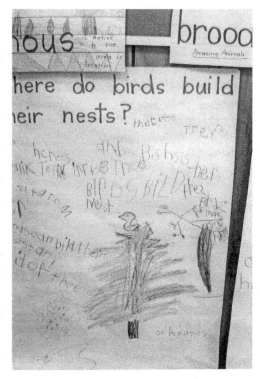

Figure 1.7

Figure 1.8 Cardinals mate for life

typically choose a bird they love or a topic like all the places birds can build nests. Figure 1.8 shows a page from a book on cardinals that uses the text features of an image and label to communicate six-year-old Andrew's expertise.

Dori's ornithology unit for kindergartners is grounded in planned learning engagements, practices that support her beliefs about teaching and learning (see Figure 1.9). More than interesting and engaging, the practices provide students the opportunity to live and learn as young ornithologists. Literacy, mathematics, and science standards are not taught or experienced in isolation, but exist as essential, collaborative skills and strategies. The universal processes of inquiry are grounded in the specifics of her unit.

Beliefs	Practices
Students need to learn how to observe birds carefully using the tools and strategies of ornithologists.	She created a bird observatory in her classroom.
Children need to learn how to pose and investigate questions from numerous perspectives.	She helped her young birders learn how to pose questions after carefully analyzing bird nests. She had students read about and quantify the birds they observed at home and at school.
Talk influences and reflects children's learning; they need to learn how to use the language of inquiry and of ornithologists.	She created a wondrous word wall to capture the language ornithologists use as demonstrated in daily read-alouds.
Scientists regularly access both primary and secondary sources when conducting formal and informal investigations.	She created a range of focused engagements using primary source data that helped her students learn how to make careful observations and interpretations.
Children need to be taught to do what scientists do.	She scaffolded students' learning to help them make observations and pose questions about what they noticed.
Scientists regularly reflect on their own learning as well as that of their colleagues. Reflection on content and processes or learning strategies promotes deeper learning and offers opportunities to teach and learn from one another.	She invited children to compose nonfiction books about birds and created class charts to show what they had learned about birds as a whole.
Children's talk during reflective conversations and responses to class questions offer honest, authentic assessment opportunities. We can find out what children have learned by paying careful attention to their formal and informal responses to class experiences.	She captured children's learning by documenting words and phrases they used when talking about birds.

Figure 1.9

▶ *A Look Inside the Classroom:* Inquiry into Ornithology

IN VIDEO CLIP 1, you'll see what Dori's classroom demonstrations look, sound, and feel like (see www.heinemann.com/products/E04603.aspx). Dori's young birders learn to read, write, and sketch as they learn to use reading, writing, and sketching to share what they are learning as ornithologists.

As you envision how to make your content and literacy instruction better reflect authentic learning in the world, consider how the processes featured in Dori's classroom might work in your own classroom. The processes of inquiry are universal because they reflect authentic learning in the world, which makes them a natural part of any unit or content area at any grade level. For more examples to inspire you, and to see how young children learn to read and interpret nonfiction text features within the context of science workshop, go online. You will also find Dori's complete unit of study on ornithology online.

Online Teaching Resources

www.heinemann.com/products/E04603.aspx
Unit 1: Ornithology, Kindergarten
Narrative 1: Teaching Nonfiction Through Ornithology Inquiry, Kindergarten
Video Clip 1: Young Ornithologists Become Authors, Kindergarten
Video Clip 2 with Transcript: Ornithologists' Circle, Kindergarten

Meeting Standards, Giving Students Choice and Ownership: Grade 4 Weather Unit

Fourth-grade teacher Brenna Osborne knew she needed to develop a unit of study around weather in response to the Science Standards. She also knew she needed to focus on nonfiction during the year in response to the English Language Arts Standards. Although many elementary teachers might view these topics as separate yet equal, Brenna recognized how they could be connected and complementary.

She could realize the potential of both sets of standards more fully and offer her students choice and ownership by creating an embedded inquiry unit on weather and nonfiction.

Brenna created a series of invitations and engagements that helped her children learn to notice and name nonfiction text features and structures, and then learn how to apply them as writers by composing nonfiction books that reflected their personal interests and wonderings about one weather concept.

Brenna knew that if students learned to think, work, and communicate as meteorologists and climatologists, they would learn the concepts described by the standards more deeply and retain their understanding longer than if they simply learned the concepts outside of authentic context and application.

Weave the Language of Inquiry and Content Vocabulary into Instruction

In minilessons and reflective conversations to wrap up workshop, like you will hear in video clip 3, it was commonplace to hear Brenna say, "That's the kind of observation a climatologist might make!" or "I wonder how a meteorologist might investigate that dilemma?" or "That surprised me. Do you think that information might help us explore climate change patterns over the past hundred years?" Because students incorporate their teacher's language into their own, the classroom community soon began talking and posing questions like meteorologists and climatologists.

The More Children Know About a Topic, the Better Their Questions Become

Inquiry is cyclical: new learning leads to new questions. To help students develop the background knowledge they need to ask good questions, Brenna created a text-set of weather-related nonfiction books. In addition, her students checked out books from the library that related to their self-selected topics.

Brenna embedded independent reading into science workshop, where students explored diverse nonfiction sources such as picture books, content literature, textbooks, and magazines with articles about weather and climate. To conclude independent reading, Brenna invited her students to share noticings about content and text structures as well as text features that nonfiction authors use. They were constructing a foundational knowledge base from which they would pose questions to guide their individual inquiries into the weather or climate topic they found most intriguing.

Brenna made space during science workshop for her students to explore the books and select those that could best help them investigate their question(s). She invited her students to pose new questions based on their latest understandings several times before settling on a question to frame their own nonfiction books.

Reading for Content and Craft

Brenna taught her students how to look at texts from different perspectives when teaching the skillfulness of inquiry, both as scientists and as writers. Although that might seem complicated, it wasn't. Brenna taught them to read like writers during demonstration/minilessons. During the workshop phase, Brenna gave them time to read nonfiction independently. As they did, Brenna asked them to keep track of what they were learning about weather as well as nonfiction text structures and features. She consistently gathered the class together after independent reading to reflect on their noticings. Whole-class reflections offered systematic opportunities for all of the students to teach and learn from one another. Brenna often captured their reflective comments on charts to permanently record what they uncovered individually and collectively. These charts served as resources for mentor text examples and structures to inform students' creation of nonfiction texts (see Figure 1.10).

When reading like writers, the fourth graders noticed the following text structures:

- Descriptions: Main ideas with details
- Sequence: Information given in order
- Questions and Answers
- Compare and Contrast

They attended to text features such as:

- How authors use headers
- How mathematics is used regularly to teach content and to emphasize points
- How models and illustrations show or synthesize narrative content
- How references and glossaries are used frequently to guide readers

---

Figure 1.10

⊙ A Look Inside the Classroom: Students Reflect on Nonfiction Text Structures and Features in Weather Books

WATCH VIDEO CLIP 3 of Brenna Osborne and her fourth graders sharing what they noticed and appreciated when they explored nonfiction texts related to their personal investigations about weather (see www.heinemann.com/products/E04603.aspx). You will see how Brenna intentionally taught thinking strategies within the context of this embedded inquiry. Reflect on the narrative of the online teaching demonstration to appreciate the depth and breadth of teaching and learning that occurred during this reflective engagement. Brenna and her students uncovered a range of text structures and features to use in their own nonfiction weather and climate books.

SCIENTIFIC READERS AND WRITERS REFLECT ON NONFICTION TEXT STRUCTURES AND FEATURES IN WEATHER BOOKS

- Look at covers and inside of books to decide what text features or structures you want to use.
- Think about what nonfiction writers do to inspire us as we write our own nonfiction.
- Use glossaries to teach vocabulary your readers may not know.
- Compose leads with facts that will draw your reader in.
- Use your guiding questions to read for particular content information.
- Choose a text structure that best fits the kind of book you are trying to write; certain questions lend themselves to particular text structures.
- Use pictures and models to embed content information.
- Be sure facts are current by checking publication dates of nonfiction materials.

The reflective conversation you witnessed by eavesdropping in the classroom through the video clip illuminates the teaching and learning potential of embedded inquiries. It also reminds us of the integral relationship between our beliefs and practices. Figure 1.11 shows how Brenna brought her beliefs to life through deliberate actions and reactions.

Brenna's Beliefs	Her Practices
We should teach students to think, work, and communicate as meteorologists and climatologists instead of simply teaching them about weather and weather forecasting.	So Brenna wove the language of inquiry and the vocabulary that climatologists and meteorologists use into minilessons and reflective sharing sessions.
The more children know about a topic, the better their questions become.	So she offered students opportunities to pose questions about climate and weather over time before settling on a burning question to frame their nonfiction books.

Figure 1.11

continues

Brenna's Beliefs	Her Practices
Students need to explore diverse nonfiction sources to construct and share current, accurate information about their topics while investigating the range of text features and structures nonfiction authors use.	So she created an extensive text-set of nonfiction books around weather, and her students checked out books from the library that connected to their self-selected topics.
We should teach students how to look at texts from different perspectives when teaching the skillfulness of inquiry.	So she invited students to investigate the books as meteorologists and climatologists when focusing on content, and as writers when noticing and naming the text features and structures used.
A workshop model should include daily demonstrations, engagements, and reflection sessions to support writers and scientists.	So she taught them to read like nonfiction writers during science workshop.
Embedded teaching shows students how to read to learn in relation to their burning questions, while also keeping an eye on the ways their nonfiction texts were constructed.	So she charted what students noticed about nonfiction text structures and features in their weather books.
It is important for students to learn how to use guiding questions when reading to learn, and it is critical to help students understand that authors make deliberate decisions so that the form of the text best supports the content or message they want to convey.	So she taught them how to select a text structure that would best suit their guiding question(s) when composing their own nonfiction books.
Teachers should notice and name moves students make to validate individual authors, and they should inspire their young colleagues to be deliberate when deciding on the content and form of their work.	So she talked with her students writer-to-writer and scientist-to-scientist.
Teachers should work in front of, alongside, and behind their students, much like an apprenticeship model.	So she composed and published a nonfiction book on weather, in front of and alongside her students.

Figure 1.11 continued

To see what Brenna's beliefs and practices look, sound, and feel like in real life with real kids, go to the online teaching resources.

Online Teaching Resources

www.heinemann.com/products/E04603.aspx
Narrative 2: Teaching Nonfiction Through Weather Inquiry, Grade 4
Video Clip 3 with Transcript: Students Reflect on Nonfiction Text Structures and Features, Grade 4

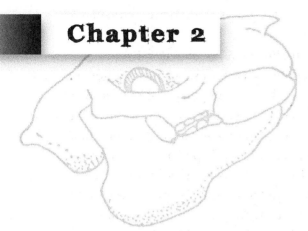

Chapter 2

Carefully Observe the World Using Tools and Strategies of the Discipline

T hink about the last time you took up something new—something you learned authentically because you were truly invested, something that meant a great deal to you personally or professionally. Reflecting on that experience, you will most likely conjure up memories that are holistic—that weave together the processes involved, information or skills learned, and your feelings about it. For the most part, content and processes are learned in concert. Often the most important moves we make and insights we generate feel almost invisible because they occur so naturally, almost magically. Yet while it may feel magical, it's not magic. It's skillful inquiry. And the more we make the processes that seem implicit explicit, the more intentional, systematic, and successful we become.

Beliefs and Practices Across Grade Levels and Content Areas

The classroom examples in this and the remaining chapters reveal the learning processes at work during integrated learning experiences. Processes that support inquiry live together symbiotically; they are neither mutually exclusive nor comprehensive.

As mutually beneficial relationships, each gives the others more power, enhancing the potential for greater impact on learning.

As we strive to create curriculum that approximates, if not directly reflects, learning in the world, it is essential that we help students learn to slow down, to notice, to look closely, and to listen carefully. When we do, we bring that sense of wonder, appreciation, and even joyful astonishment back into children's lives. As physicist Ben Brabson puts it so aptly, "The beauty of approaching a scientific problem, first you become a marvelous observer of the world around you" (personal communication, 1996). This stance isn't unique to scientists. During focused inquiries, we make observations using the tools and strategies designed to investigate questions related to the particular discipline. As we learned from Dori and her young ornithologists, birders use tools such as binoculars and sketchbooks to capture bird sightings, chart the frequency of those sightings, and identify migration patterns within and between regions. Historians carefully analyze photos, print sources (including newspapers), songs, artwork, personal letters, and formal records to reconstruct the stories of the people and events in various time periods. Making space for formal and informal observations (giving students simple tools such as a magnifying glass), having students record their observations (visually or in writing), letting them talk about what they observe, and supplementing their observations with informational books is all that's needed.

Ask, "What Do You Notice?"

Years ago Carolyn Burke shone a light on the role of observation and questioning in genuine inquiry. She taught us that observation unites all disciplines. All learning, regardless of content, begins with careful, systematic observation. Authors notice people, places, and interactions and jot down their observations in a writer's notebook. Often these noticings become seed ideas that grow into masterpieces. Mathematicians observe patterns in nature, in architecture, on number charts, and so on. Artists develop an eye for observing, appreciating, and capturing the aesthetic. Naturalists pay attention to animal footprints, tree markings, and insect trails when observing the flora and fauna of a region. When we teach children to think about and work in a discipline, we need to begin with observation.

Kindergarten/first-grade teacher Jennifer Barnes notes that the most important question she asks children is, "What do you notice?" She puts children in a position to make careful observations and then opens the conversation with this guiding question, the most common one asked by those of us who teach through inquiry. Children need to learn how to slow down and focus on specific details, and then we can help them learn to question and explore. Teachers notice and name the kind of observations or questions children pose, connecting what a child says to a particular way of viewing the world or discipline. Comments like "That's the kind of question a biologist would ask" help steer children toward other observations and questions. The content areas (as we call them in school) or disciplines (as we call them in the professional world) are differentiated by the nature of the observations and questions posed. Different disciplines investigate different kinds of questions. Philosophers wonder about the principles by which people should conduct their lives, anthropologists inquire into cultures, and geographers explore the ways people adjust to their environments (Short and Burke 1991).

Children will understand concepts better if we teach them how to observe and generate questions from the perspectives of the various disciplines and then give them the tools developed to answer those questions. The story of Galileo Galilei, as told by Peter Sis in *Starry Messenger* (1996), illustrates this process. Galileo spent much time intensely observing the heavens with the naked eye. After learning of an instrument that had been invented to see things far away, he constructed one for himself. "Night after night, he gazed through his telescope and wrote down everything he observed. Then he published his observations in a book which he called *Starry Messenger*" (14). By observing, asking questions, finding the right tool to investigate these questions, and then recording his deductions, Galileo furthered our understanding of astronomy. This led others to generate new questions, prompting the development of new instruments. We can trace our current NASA space exploration technologies to the construction of a simple tool, the telescope, which opened the heavens to human exploration, challenged status quo thinking, and demonstrated that the earth was not the center of the universe.

Teaching children that knowledge is tentative—not static but constantly evolving—is essential. Because what we know will change, we want our students to spend as much time learning *how* to learn as they do learning what we currently know. This way they can better question and contribute to the existing knowledge.

Make Careful Observations

One of the most compelling ways early childhood teachers can help students learn to slow down and make careful observations is to put a camera in their hands. Several years ago K–1 teacher Jennifer Barnes and parent Robin Thomas created a "storybook garden," with sections that reflect themes, settings, or characters of touchstone texts like *Listen to the Wind* (Mortenson and Roth 2009), *The Quilt Maker's Gift* (Brumbeau 2001), *Make Way for Ducklings* (McCloskey 1999), and *The Hello, Goodbye Window* (Juster 2005). K–1 classes use the garden for independent reading, writing workshop, and science and math investigations. Students in grades 2 through 5 are invited to use the garden as well, to live and learn in a lovely, natural setting.

The storybook garden has grown into an exquisite and productive natural teaching space. Jennifer's budding photographers carefully explore the garden to find just the right spot to take a photo, emulating those of professional nature photographers such as Ansel Adams, whose work they have explored in class. After children have taken a photo, Jennifer and her teaching assistant, Lisa Smith, ask them to suggest a title for the photograph and provide "about the photographer" information. The title, photographer's name, and a blurb are typed on an exhibit card displayed under the photograph (see Figure 2.1).

This activity, along with the photography exhibit, showcases the value of noticing and naming the world. It fosters the development of children who identify themselves as careful, thoughtful observers who lead delightfully diverse lives.

Masterpiece Title: "Fun of A Leaf"
Photographer: Carey, 6 years old
About the Photographer: Carey enjoys going outside to play basketball. He has taken 12 or 15 pictures before.

Masterpiece Title: "Green Sparkle Dropper"
Photographer: Emery, 5 years old
About the Photographer: Emery enjoys playing with her neighbors' puppies named Jojo and Lola. She has taken many pictures before with her very own camera.

Figure 2.1

Carefully Observe History by Interpreting Primary Source Photographs and Artifacts

Photographs of people and places across space and time are compelling invitations for careful observation. Whole- and small-group investigations of primary source photographs are an especially powerful way to launch a unit of study or mini-inquiry in the social sciences.

Fifth-grade teacher Tameka Breland inspires her students to explore immigration and the critical issues that surround it by examining Ellis Island photos. She asks her students to look closely at a photograph and jot down what they notice. Then she gives them a few minutes to share their thinking with a partner. After everyone has expressed her or his ideas, the class generates a list of general observations about the photographs. Having exploratory conversations about the photos piques the children's curiosity, such that their observations and wonderings became increasingly sophisticated as they build on one another's ideas.

Tameka uses these initial observations and questions as a touchstone throughout the unit, giving students opportunities to expand, refine, and revise their original thinking. On a given day they may discuss an immigration article during their morning meeting, explore during writing workshop how writers of historical fiction use primary resources to gather information, and generate statements capturing their current beliefs about immigrants during social studies workshop (the content area generating the inquiry). They read and discuss books such as *The Orphan of Ellis Island* (Woodruff 2000), *Grandmother and the Runaway Shadow* (Rosenberg 1996), *Letters from Rifka* (Hesse 2009), *A House of Tailors* (Giff 2006), *Nory Ryan's Song* (Giff 2002), and *The Lotus Seed* (Garland 1997) in literature circles.

Tameka weaves in additional opportunities to look closely at primary sources connected to immigration in the past and present, using both replicas of original artifacts and online images.

When we ask children to explore primary source documents—photos, sketches, videos, or texts—we teach them how to think and work as historians or archeologists. They generate hunches, share them with their fellow inquirers, consult additional sources, and then rethink and revise. In this way, we are not telling children what to think; rather, we are teaching them how to think for themselves and how to ground their interpretations in data.

A few years ago Tameka and I created a template for the immigration unit of study (see Figure 2.2), which can be easily adapted for any grade level or topic. I use it with graduate students, and Tameka uses it with fourth and fifth graders. It promotes careful observation and critical thinking so that students intentionally outgrow their initial understanding. The guiding questions inspire students to make inferences, cross-check data, pay careful attention to detail, and question what they think they know.

Inquiry into Immigration

Name_____ Date:_____

Focus of inquiry:_____
(book, newspaper article, Internet site, artifact, and its connection to immigration)

Respond to this question before you examine the artifact or text:
What do I think I know?

Respond to the next two questions as you interpret the artifact or text:
What do I notice?

What does it mean?

Respond to the last question after you reflect on the artifact or reading:
What surprised me most?

Complete after your conversation around the artifact or text:
I used to believe . . .

Now I think . . .

Figure 2.2

We have our tall and small teachers/learners complete the first question before engaging with the artifact or text. Then they complete the next three questions independently on the basis of careful observation and interpretation. Next, they talk with partners or in small groups to discover their colleagues' perspectives. Finally, they complete the remaining two sentences, which are designed to push them to revisit their initial beliefs.

These guiding questions help students make sense of what they have before them, just as historians do. Historians do not passively accept sterilized versions of reality; instead, they construct thick interpretative descriptions after intensively combing through stories, songs, artwork, formal and informal records, photos, tools, artifacts, and structures. Learning to slow down—to focus and make careful observations—is the foundation for deep, abiding understanding.

Learning Observation Through Sketching

Sketching sounds so simple, and it is. Yet it is one of the best ways to help children learn how to look and how to convey what they notice. Sketching requires a level of attention and careful consideration that exceeds a quick glance or two. We see in new ways and ask new questions with pencils and sketch pads in our hands.

Many teachers consider sketchbooks to be one of their most important teaching tools. They order them at the beginning of the year along with writer's notebooks, pens, pencils, glue sticks, and facial tissue. Sometimes a whole class will carefully observe and sketch something together—a tree on the school grounds, for example—but children can also choose the items they sketch. Sketching stretches our thinking and helps students attend to the parts in relation to the whole.

Students in Melissa Klosterman's kindergarten/first-grade classroom are given space to explore daily. She makes sure that her invitations to explore nudge children forward as readers, writers, mathematicians, scientists, and social scientists. These explorations include sketching because Melissa knows it's a fundamental inquiry process. Her science area is filled with interesting artifacts: some are living and breathing specimens (frogs and toads, spiders, butterflies) and others reflect what once was alive (fossils, skulls, skeletons, dead leaves). Melissa's novice scientists try their hand at capturing their observations of these artifacts in a sketch (see Figure 2.3). They often consult informational texts to help them understand what they see, and they use mathematics to quantify and convey what they notice.

Jennifer Barnes considers sketching to be so foundational to children's love of learning and enriched understanding that she devotes time to teaching them to sketch just as she teaches them to write. Mentor artists like Jan Brett (in a video) give

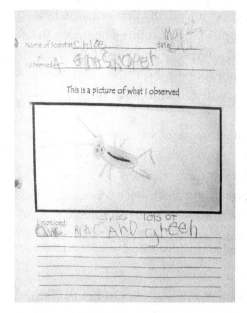

Figure 2.3 Grasshopper Sketch

Figure 2.4 Trevor's Sketch Inspired by Jan Brett

Jennifer's young artists sketching lessons. Jennifer tracks their growth as artists just as she chronicles their development as authors—and that growth is astonishing. Trevor, a first grader, was so inspired that he shared his sketches with Jan Brett when she spoke at a local bookstore in Columbia, SC. His work (see Figure 2.4) underscores the value of teaching children how to look and capture what they see.

Second/third-grade teacher Tim O'Keefe builds on the rich sketching experiences his students have had in their K–1 classrooms: Students learn to sketch an object from different perspectives, including labels and using a measuring tape for accuracy. We deepen children's appreciation of the world and the content they are exploring when we slow learning down enough so that children can notice, name, and learn for themselves.

Make Time and Space for Careful Observations in Your Classroom

The most important thing you can do as a teacher is to provide space and time for your students to learn—as readers, writers, mathematicians, scientists, social scientists, artists, and musicians. Observation is at the heart of each discipline's way of knowing the world. Because we live in a fast-food, video-game culture, many children need to build their observational skills and stamina. It's worth the investment when you have students who can notice carefully, name and describe accurately, and wonder about their observations; this process is central to effective learning within and across disciplines.

There are probably other areas of your curriculum that you could enhance by building in more time for careful observation. Begin by planning ways to incorporate photography and sketching into your units. Think of times when your children can take and interpret photos or convey their interpretations of things they observe by sketching. A classroom camera, a printer, and blank paper are all you need to get started. Scaffolding is important to success in the classroom; whether you are helping students learn to take photos, interpret photos, or sketch, begin with whole-class activities and provide steps toward independence. For example:

- Show children how you would capture a scene as a photographer by thinking aloud about your composition, and then let a few kids try it. Have them share their strategies as well as their final products. When teaching how to interpret photos, think aloud as you share what you notice and wonder about; then, invite the kids to add to your list and create a chart for everyone to refer to. With all the new classroom technologies at our disposal, it's easy to pull up photos or primary sources on Smart Boards for the whole class to examine.
- To tap into the power of sketching, introduce your students to picture book illustrators or naturalists who capture the world in sketches, and carefully examine the moves they make, just as you would ask kids to notice and name the authors' writing crafts (Ray 1999). Once kids have shown a genuine appreciation for sketching, have them sit in a circle and sketch an object you've put in the center. As they sketch, have them describe their process to a partner. After a few minutes, invite them to share strategies that are working and struggles they are encountering. Help them recognize that sketching is like writing: Envisioning and revision are both integral to the process. Emphasize how much they are learning by looking so closely and exploring the relationship between the parts and the whole.

Slowing down takes lots of practice for children and adults alike. Once you devote focused time to it, everything else you do works better. It's like building community: The more time you put into establishing a productive, efficient, and caring group, the less time you have to spend on classroom management. This is why helping students become careful observers using tools and strategies of the discipline is a foundational process, one that takes time and patience to grow, one that enhances all the others.

Chapter 3

Pose and Investigate Questions from Numerous Perspectives

A s we strive to create curriculum that approximates, if not directly reflects, learning in the world, it is essential that we help students learn to shift perspectives. You're aware of the sage advice that how we look influences what we see. This applies in school and out. As Marcel Proust put it so eloquently, "The real voyage of discovery consists not in seeking new landscapes but in having new eyes."

Consider Whose Voice Is Being Heard

Proust's words underpin the need to help students pose and investigate questions from varied perspectives. When we teach children to look at the world—as readers, writers, mathematicians, scientists, social scientists, artists, and musicians—we deepen and broaden their learning simultaneously. When we ask who created the information and for what audience, we help our students understand that knowledge isn't neutral; it can be biased. When we ask why the information matters in the world or why it matters to us, we help our students contextualize and personalize new understanding. When we ask, "So what?" and "Now what?" we urge children to act on what they've learned. The questions we ask determine the answers we find.

Take a topic—the Civil War, for instance. What we now understand about that tragic time in our history reflects many perspectives. We often give historians full credit. Yet while it's true they've made incredible contributions, they didn't act alone. They consulted people in other disciplines to construct their interpretations—among them archeologists and economists, anthropologists and sociologists, politicians and theologians, and artists of all sorts—and offer unique yet complementary perspectives on the people, places, and events. What a difference it makes to ask, "Whose voice is heard? Whose voice is missing?" when interrogating texts about the Civil War. Are African Americans included in the narrative? What about women—where were they, and what were they doing at that time and at that place? When we consider issues from diverse points of view, we are seeking to understand for ourselves by putting together the pieces of the puzzle. When we invite kids to intentionally pose and investigate questions from numerous perspectives, we are teaching them how to learn while enhancing what they are learning.

This process repositions students, from passively receiving information to actively constructing, owning, and acting on their learning. Consider the poster from Brandon Foote's second-grade class, shown in Figure 3.1, which was created by his students to represent their vision for a new class museum.

Brandon has clearly sent the message to his students that learning history is so much more than memorizing dates and facts. He has helped them recognize that they learn about their past as a way to actively build a better

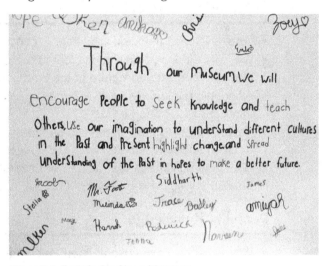

Figure 3.1 Beliefs for Class Museum

future. They know they are both teachers and learners. They know they should seek to understand others. They know knowledge is power if we live it out in our own lives. They know they actively construct, not simply receive, information. Notice the language these second graders chose to use: *encourage, seek, teach, use, highlight, spread, make.*

One simple yet effective way to ensure that children learn how to pose and investigate questions from varied perspectives is to offer guiding questions to consider that relate to the topic. Reflecting on the kinds of questions I noticed teachers using to promote genuine inquiry, I have organized them by topic and grade level in this chapter. Different units of study call for different questions, of course. Figure 3.2 illustrates the ways questions help us frame and investigate our world.

Conceptual

- *Perspectives:* Which perspectives (reader, writer, mathematician, scientist, and/or social scientist) offer potential insights or strategies for investigating this topic? (What questions would a social scientist or a mathematician ask and how might they investigate this issue?)
- *Systems:* What systems are involved and how are they related?
- *Cycles:* Are there embedded cycles? How might we gain a deeper understanding of this topic by investigating natural and man-made cycles?
- *Change:* Has change occurred over time in relation to this topic? If so, how might studying the natural or man-made changes help us better understand the topic?
- *Voice:* Whose voice is heard or privileged? Whose voice is absent or silenced?
- *Power:* How might power structures help us better understand this issue?

Pragmatic/Universal

- Who developed the idea, invention, or concept?
- Why was the idea or invention created? What was the purpose of the invention given the context and culture of the time period?
- Where did the knowledge or information presented in the materials we are exploring come from? Can we trust it?
- Have we selected varied sources of information (primary and secondary) to broaden and verify our knowledge or understanding?
- Have common knowledge, beliefs, or understanding about this topic changed over time? If so, what led to these shifts?

Personal Knowledge

- Why does this knowledge or information matter to me?
- How has what I have learned changed me?

Social Knowledge

- Why does the knowledge I'm learning matter in the world?

From Personal Knowledge to Social Action

- So why does this matter?
- Now what? How might we take action on what we have learned?
- How might we show or demonstrate what we have learned to others?

Figure 3.2 Guiding Questions

Beliefs and Practices Across Grade Levels and Content Areas

The classroom explorations that follow demonstrate diverse yet powerful ways to promote this process of helping children pose and investigate questions from varied perspectives (readers, writers, mathematicians, scientists, social scientists, artists, and musicians). You will also see how organizing curriculum around a broad concept like "systems," a foundational concept in the sciences and social sciences, helps students better understand unique perspectives and relationships with other disciplines. Finally, you will see how teaching children to pose and investigate diverse questions is central to adopting a critical stance, one that leads kids to question the status quo. When children make a habit of asking critical questions, they develop a sense of agency by taking action on new knowledge and developing the imagination to embrace possibilities that might not be presented to them by the larger, dominant culture.

What Kinds of Questions Might We Ask About Trees and How Might We Investigate Them? *(K–1 unit of study)*

GUIDING QUESTIONS

- What kinds of questions do readers, writers, mathematicians, artists, and scientists ask about trees?
- How might we investigate trees as readers, writers, mathematicians, artists, and scientists?
- What are the tools that readers, writers, mathematicians, artists, and scientists use and how might they help us learn about trees?

Children acquire the habit of inquiry by participating in many investigations over time. K–1 teacher Dori Gilbert began creating yearlong inquiries in order to meet the science standards in ways that would bring them to life. The overview of South Carolina's science standards for kindergarten argue for this kind of teaching: "The focus of science in kindergarten is to provide students with hands-on experiences that will utilize their natural curiosity at the beginning of their development of scientific knowledge. Kindergarten students need to expand their observation skills as they learn about the life, earth, and physical sciences" (South Carolina Department of Education 2005, 6). Using the picture book *Sky Tree* (Locker 1995) as inspiration, Dori designed a series of invitations throughout the year to help children become careful and passionate observers in and outside school. This curriculum was so successful that all the

K–1 teachers at the Center for Inquiry use it now. If you are a first grader at CFI, you can count on monthly opportunities to investigate a tree in the schoolyard or one in your own backyard.

Teachers launch the project by reading *Sky Tree* aloud. The book illustrates the unique yet interrelated ties between art and science. In the author's note, Thomas Locker writes:

> *I have spent most of my life learning to paint trees against the ever changing sky. I still cannot look at a tree without being filled with a sense of wonder. Since I began collaborating with Candace Christiansen, who is a science teacher, I have become increasingly aware of the scientific approach to the natural world. I was amazed to discover that the more scientific facts I learned, the deeper my sense of wonder became. This realization led to the creation of* Sky Tree.

Locker and Christiansen's process when creating the book reflects the way we want our students to work—through collaborative, cross-content investigations that merge art and science, which ultimately produce exemplary final products.

After reading the book aloud, the teachers and children explore the school grounds to find a tree they want to adopt as their class "sky tree" for the year. Then they visit the tree, often at first, each time looking at it from a different perspective. They bring paint, chalk, or colored pencils and their sketchbook to capture the tree as artists. They bring measuring tape and graph paper to examine the tree as mathematicians. They bring their writer's notebook to jot down wondrous words that capture what the tree looks like and then write a poetic description of it. They learn to wonder about trees and how to select tools created by different disciplines to explore their questions.

Jennifer Barnes devotes a week or so to leaf investigations in the fall. Each area in her classroom is devoted to helping the children look at leaves from a different perspective. They investigate leaves through the lens of a mathematician, a scientist and author, and an artist (see Figure 3.3).

When the teachers feel that students are invested in the process of looking at a tree from various perspectives, the children can take the learning home. Each child chooses a tree in her or his own yard or neighborhood. Then, in monthly homework assignments, they capture the ways in which the tree changes during the school year. Teachers offer guiding questions or suggestions such as, "Think about how your tree has changed since you started observing it. What do you notice about the cycles that trees go through as they grow and change? Show the changes as an artist in a series of sketches and as an author using descriptive words." The students bring their products to school and they are all added to a class display in a special area of the classroom (see Figure 3.4).

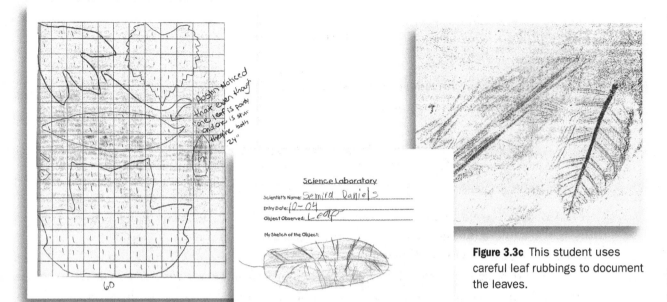

Figure 3.3a Austin captures and documents leaves as a mathematician, counting blocks to compare the size of different-shaped leaves, foundational experiences around the concept of area.

Figure 3.3c This student uses careful leaf rubbings to document the leaves.

Figure 3.3b Semira takes a scientific look at leaves using art and language to describe different properties.

Figure 3.4 Observations of Trees Over Time

Explore South Carolina *(summer project, prior to third grade)*

GUIDING QUESTIONS

- How might we investigate South Carolina as readers, writers, mathematicians, musicians, artists, scientists, historians, and sociologists?
- What artifacts might we collect when visiting different places in our state over the summer in order to create a museum about South Carolina when we return to school as third graders?

In South Carolina, the social studies curriculum is devoted almost entirely to an investigation of the state. Unfortunately, the typical curriculum resources devised to teach about the state don't begin to capture its beauty, complex history, diverse heritage, and geography. Second/third-grade teacher Susanne Pender developed this particular unit of study to meet the third-grade social studies standards, accomplishing that and so much more. She envisioned a unit of study that would offer students choice and voice while intentionally and systematically learning how to use reading, writing, mathematics, music, and art as tools for learning about South Carolina as scientists and social scientists. To bring the curriculum to life in lasting ways, she created a homework project to be completed during the summer between second and third grade. (Susanne moves with her students from second to third grade, but this project is also viable when the students have different teachers each year, as long as the teachers involved buy in and participate.)

At the end of second grade Susanne sends a journal home with her students as an end-of-year gift, providing directions for its use in a "Survival Kit for the Inquirer" (see Figure 3.5). It includes examples of the ways children might use the journal to chronicle what they learn about South Carolina while vacationing, visiting relatives, or simply exploring their home community. Susanne tells them they can collect information for their project anywhere in South Carolina, from their backyard to the Blue Ridge Mountains to the Atlantic Ocean: "The important thing to remember is to observe, record, and think about the world around you." To remind students of the importance of using guiding questions when inquiring, Susanne lists the various perspectives (scientist, author/reader, mathematician, sociologist, artist), or *lenses*, they might look through when noticing, naming, and wondering about their world. During the summer they collect artifacts (rocks, insects, leaves, soil samples, travel brochures, photos, books by South Carolina authors, and so on) and capture what they notice in their journals.

Inquiring About South Carolina!

How much do you know about the state in which we live?

The state of South Carolina is one of the most interesting and unique places in our country. Our big idea of study in the third grade will focus on growth and change, from the history and characteristics of South Carolina to our personal roles as learners. This summer project will help us begin to look closely at our world as we plan and travel this summer and get us off to a wonderful start in the fall!

What: With these ideas in mind, I would like to invite you to use your travels and experiences this summer to help collect information and artifacts for an exploration project.

Why: The purpose of this activity is to gather information on South Carolina while thinking in a variety of perspectives in order to enhance our upcoming units of study throughout the next school year. Some of these units include rocks and minerals, the history of our state, native artists and musicians, people who have made an impact on our state, and governmental structures.

How: You can . . .

- Write reflections, facts, memories, and stories in your journal.
- Take pictures and write captions that explain where, when, what, and why.
- Create illustrations and art work.
- Gather artifacts such as pamphlets, maps, graphs, information from books, newspapers, or postcards.

Bring this information back to school in August to help us get started on our in-depth study.

When/Where: Information for this project can be created or collected anywhere in South Carolina, from your backyard, to the mountains, or even the beach! The important thing to remember is to observe, record, and think about the world around you. If you are visiting other states over the summer, I invite you to look closely and find ways you can compare differences and similarities between the state you are visiting and South Carolina.

I have listed some of the perspectives below that you can look through while thinking about your world. These are some suggestions to get you started, and I look forward to seeing the directions you take while exploring and investigating for this project!

Figure 3.5

continues

Thinking like a . . .

Scientist	Social Scientist and Historian (someone who studies people and the past)
Plants/animals	Key events and people in S.C.'s history
Weather	History of a certain region
Insects	History and characteristics of a culture (Gullah, for example)
Natural resources	Ways people make a living or have fun in different places
Water	Current events that affect S.C.
Soil/land formations	Government
Inquiry exploration	Historic buildings and places

Author/Reader	Artist
Stories from the past as a part of family or cultural history	Music from past and present
Stories or books based on S.C.	Paintings
Stories set in S.C.	Dances like the "Shag"
Original writing that ties to S.C.	Drama
Authors that are from S.C.	Artists from S.C.

Mathematician
Population of places over time
Graphs and data found in the newspaper, like baseball statistics for a S.C. team
Any charts or graphs that focus on presenting information about S.C.

Happy hunting and have a wonderful summer!

Figure 3.5 continued

Susanne also offers guidance for parents so they understand the purpose of the summer project. Parents play a key role in helping their children complete the assignment. Susanne puts it this way in a newsletter:

In third grade, our state and district standards focus on our students' ability to investigate and learn about important aspects of South Carolina. We will explore our state as historians, botanists, geologists, authors, social and political scientists, and even mathematicians. The purpose of this summer project is to gather knowledge and artifacts based on our collective experiences during this time. All information gathered will be placed into a collective South Carolina exhibit that we will work with throughout the year.

One of the first things the students do as third graders is set up a South Carolina museum using the artifacts they collect over the summer (see Figure 3.6).

They organize the museum by categories: rocks and soil samples; plants; insects; brochures and stories about the cultures of South Carolina; charts, maps, and graphs that reveal statistics about the state; and so on. Each child also becomes an expert on a particular area of South Carolina and makes a presentation to the class. For example:

Figure 3.6 Students Collect Artifacts

- Sheldon accompanied his dad to work, at a hydropower plant on Lake Murray. He took pictures, drew a diagram of the turbines, showed how hydroelectricity is used, and gave facts about the history of the lake. He displayed this information on a poster.
- Colin videotaped a family outing on Lake Murray and showed how Purple Martins, birds native to this area, returned to one specific island each night at dusk. His narration called attention to different plants and animals found in or near the lake, as well as recreational activities taking place in or on the water. He told about the Hydrilla infestation the lake was experiencing at the time and the ways naturalists were trying to correct the problem. His video was viewed again and again as the class discussed the migration of animals, man's influence on natural habitats, and the concept of cause and effect.

- Jay loved rocks and minerals, so he spent a great deal of time collecting rocks and doing research. He took notes about his findings in his rock journal and included a picture with each entry. Whenever his family visited other areas of South Carolina, he gathered new specimens and added them to his collection. His collection and journal were consulted many times during a unit on rocks and minerals.

- Matt's father worked for the South Carolina Geological Alliance and was able to collect rock and soil samples from various regions of the state. They became a valuable set of resources during a unit of study on the earth and prompted a mini-inquiry into the types of soil found throughout Congaree Swamp National Park.

- Hayden's family visited the beach. After collecting a gallon of seawater, he and his mother conducted a number of experiments. In one, Hayden boiled some of the ocean water down to leave the remaining salt. Hayden gave a wonderful presentation on the difference between salt water and fresh water and the animals he found in salt water.

- During a family gathering in Beaufort, Zakiya visited the nearby Gullah settlement. She created a PowerPoint presentation in which she described the Gullah culture: its history, way of life, and unique language. A website she found was a great source of information when the class discussed the various cultures within South Carolina.

- Abhinav looked at the world as a mathematician, so he researched the demographics of the various counties. His chart included number of residents, percentage of unemployment, and natural resources. Susanne used this chart during a morning warm-up to introduce how numbers are used in the world and to talk about percentages.

- Teal kept a chronological travel diary/photo album—trips to her grandparents' home in the country, a visit to Carowinds (an amusement park), her days at the beach, and her adventure with a group of naturalists as they watched sea turtles hatch and crawl to the ocean in the moonlight. Her thoughts, observations, illustrations, pictures, pamphlets, and artifacts all helped communicate her experiences. The children's questions about the sea turtles led to an in-depth inquiry about the creatures during a unit of study on animals.

This project brings new energy to the curriculum. Each child's perspective reflects his or her learning experiences and shows how important it is to look at the same landscape through different lenses. After the South Carolina museum is created and expert presentations have been made, Susanne uses the museum as a curricular touchstone throughout the year to help students make connections between the known and the new. The class begins their inquiry into geology with rocks and soil housed in the museum, and their culture studies by revisiting the cultures represented in the museum. The South Carolina museum becomes an authentic reference.

Explore Systems of the Body and How They Are Related
(first-grade unit of study)

GUIDING QUESTIONS

- What do the systems of the body do? How do they work?
- How do systems of the body all work together? How are they connected?
- What do we need to know to take good care of ourselves?

Although many first-grade classrooms limit teaching about the body to reviewing the senses and basic body parts, kids are capable of learning so much more. First-grade teachers Melissa Klosterman and Jennifer Barnes organize a unit of study around the systems by which the body functions. This shift in perspective transforms teaching and learning opportunities. Major strands of medicine have grown out of a systems approach to the human body—this is how professionals learn, and it works just as beautifully in the classroom. Students gather information from primary sources—X-rays, personal experiences, lots of rich nonfiction texts. They learn about the parts of the body and how they work by asking questions about and exploring the digestive, respiratory, circulatory, musculoskeletal, and nervous systems.

Explore the Idea of General Systems *(second-grade unit of study)*

GUIDING QUESTIONS

- How can understanding the idea of systems provide children with a tool for learning about their world and help make connections among all areas of learning?
- What is the difference between a system and a cycle? Are they connected? Are certain systems interdependent?
- What are the types of systems, including man-made/natural, closed/open, living/nonliving?
- How can knowing about systems help us when approaching large projects or personal goals?

Second-grade teacher Susanne Pender makes explicit connections to the knowledge about bodily systems children construct in first grade in a unit that explores systems in general. Susanne explains the beliefs that underpin the unit:

When inquiring about the world and ourselves, an invaluable tool for learning is having the ability to look at a large system and identify/understand the smaller parts or steps which must come together to reach a goal or make something happen.

When children notice and name the components and individual jobs within a given system and see how they all fit together, they begin to apply this understanding by looking at a variety of situations from different perspectives.

Children appreciate a sense of order and are naturally interested in knowing how things work. An inquiry into systems builds on a child's natural curiosity and promotes questions while sparking new investigations. These investigations lead to making connections to and within other systems while fostering more questions and a deeper level of understanding.

She launches the inquiry by reading aloud *Gifted Hands: The Ben Carson Story* (Carson and Murphey 1996). She shares the guiding questions of the unit explicitly and provides daily opportunities to discuss them during morning meetings and in her science/social studies workshop. Talking about the book, students revisit and build on their current understanding of bodily systems, especially the nervous system. After the read-aloud, Susanne presents a lesson using the game Mouse Trap. She also takes her students on a field trip to a local restaurant during this "percolation period," during which they document all the systems that work together within the larger system.

Then the students step back, reflect, create a working definition of a system, and begin documenting their ideas, observations, and questions on a touchstone chart (see

Figure 3.7) that is consulted and added to throughout the unit. Morning meetings provide a forum for kids to make connections by sharing their questions and building on one another's ideas.

Susanne deliberately yet fluidly moves from natural, living systems to man-made systems such as blood banks and hospitals. Using a range of demonstrations and engagements, Susanne teaches students how to notice, and name, living and nonliving systems and common characteristics of systems. Then the class investigates the systems that work together in a bicycle.

The kids start to notice systems everywhere; they go beyond simply noticing and naming systems. They learn to ask how systems work, how they are connected, how to generalize from one system to another, and how to differentiate between open and closed as well as living and nonliving systems (see Figure 3.8). As Proust put it, "They learn to look at the landscape of their lives with new eyes."

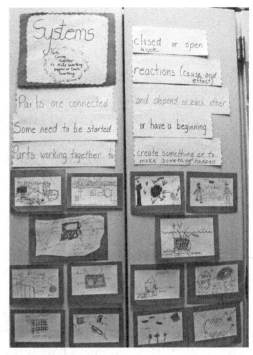

Figure 3.7 Student Observations on Systems

Observations Made While Exploring a Variety of Systems

1. **Other factors can affect a system in both positive and negative ways.**
   Examples:
   - pollution in an ecosystem
   - using certain chemicals to clean and filter water during treatment
2. **Systems connect to other systems or within a larger system.**
   water system—farming system—shipping of food—restaurants
3. **If you know how one system works, you may understand another one better.**
   body systems: nervous, immune, skeletal, etc.
4. **Some systems are closed, like a cycle, and others are open ended. Some are living and some are nonliving systems.**
   Living: photosynthesis, life cycle of insects
   Nonliving: crop rotation, engines

Figure 3.8 Conclusions Students Made About a Variety of Systems

After Susanne is confident her students can identify and explore a range of systems, she invites each of them to choose a system she or he wants to understand better. The assignment and topic choices are shown in Figure 3.9. Note the diversity of topic choices that foster a deep understanding of the conceptual nature of systems. The presentations enrich the class's understanding of systems in general and show that the systems that surround the children's lives are interconnected. Systems are everywhere!

Pose Critical Questions: Opinion Writing and Persuasive Essays on Zoos (second- and third-grade unit of study)

GUIDING QUESTIONS

- Who developed the idea of zoos?
- Why were zoos invented or created? What was the purpose of the invention given the context and culture of the time period?
- Have common knowledge, beliefs, or understandings about zoos changed over time? What led to shifts in our beliefs or understandings?
- Why do zoos matter to me?
- How has what I have learned about zoos during this unit changed me?

Second-/third-grade teacher Chris Hass is passionate about teaching children how to adopt a critical stance when investigating topics in and outside of school. He also believes in teaching responsively. He takes into account his students' interests and questions when crafting his lesson plans. He carefully and strategically negotiates his vision for curriculum on the basis of what emerges during classroom conversations and explorations. He teaches kids to think critically by having them undertake mini-inquiries around compelling topics they themselves have raised. One of the most important aspects of his approach to critical literacy is pushing kids to question what their particular culture or society at large considers to be normal.

Most second and third graders have never considered questioning their opinion of zoos. In their experience, zoos are fun and entertaining, and are places that take good care of animals. Adults' opinions about zoos are not always as positive, but Chris doesn't impose his perspective; he helps students learn to deliberately shift perspective on a topic and come to a new, informed position. He describes the evolution of the zoo inquiry this way:

> After reading that a coyote that had been victimizing neighborhood dogs might be relocated to a zoo, the class began wondering where the animals in zoos come from. This led them to wonder what life was like for the animals in the zoo enclosures. As

Our class definition of a *system:* different parts of something working together to make something happen or to create something. Each part has a particular job to do and comes together. Can be in nature or man-made.

Now that we have investigated the concept of systems over the past few weeks, it's time to choose a system you find interesting and investigate it for a personal inquiry. After using your skills as a researcher, you will take the role of teacher and share your new knowledge with your classmates.

Requirements for expert project:

- Brainstorm ideas and think about how it will be in the end. (Visualize what it could be.)
- Create a list of questions you would like to answer through your investigation.
- Include at least ten facts that help explain how it works, what it does, what parts are involved and how each one works, and how the parts are connected.
- The project needs to have a model/visual to show how it works.
- Do it on something you are interested in learning.
- Present information in a booklet, on a poster, using technology, or any way that will help you teach your system to your classmates.
- Talk about how it may be part of a larger system.
- Look at the system through the eyes of a historian. How has the system changed over time?
- How has this new information changed the way you look at your world? What new questions do you have now?
- Gather and organize your information on note cards.

Be ready to turn in all evidence of the different stages of work, including note cards and first and final drafts. (We will take these things step by step during writing workshop.)

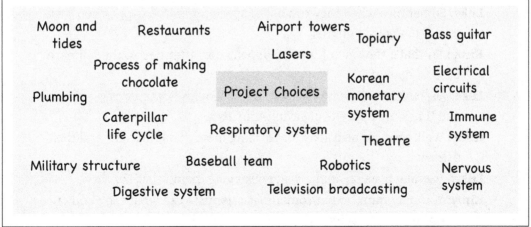

Figure 3.9 Systems Assignment and Topic Choices

they read more and more they found that many sources were writing and sharing facts with an agenda in mind—to defend or attack zoos. These sources used only the facts that supported their stance, leaving out the others.

The kids tried to think about this problem from a variety of perspectives. They chose a perspective (elephant, three year old, mom, animal activist, zoologist) and tried to think about what these different groups would say about zoos. After learning a good deal about animals' natural habitats (their wants and needs) and also about zoos, the kids had a written conversation/debate with a parent or sibling. They let the parent/sibling choose the side of the argument she or he felt most passionately about, then took the other side themselves.

The conversation that follows between two siblings illustrates the kind of thinking that is both possible and desirable when teachers help children shift perspectives and learn to think critically by questioning what, up until now, they have considered normal. A written conversation like this is a natural scaffold to opinion/argument writing.

Kirby: I think zoos are good because they help save animal populations like the California condor. They used breeding programs to help raise these birds' population numbers from nearly two dozen birds to a whole lot more. What about that!

Luke: The spaces they give the animals are so small that they have no room to run so they get fat.

Kirby: Well either way you can obviously see that zoos are good because they also rescue animals that are hurt, like two baby polar bear cubs.

Luke: Sometimes when they run out of space for an animal in a zoo they feed it to another animal.

Kirby: So that's the way of life. It happens day after day in the animal's natural habitat.

Luke: Yes, but the only thing you have talked about is how zoos save animals and that's the opposite of saving animals.

Kirby: Well, zoos are also good for learning more about animals and their behavior.

Luke: Running tests on animals and observing them is bad for them.

Kirby: You may think so but sometimes scientists use what they find out to make new medicines.

Chris uses embedded inquiries to meet a range of standards efficiently and effectively across content areas. To launch the embedded inquiry, he does what we have learned to do from leaders in our field like Katie Wood Ray and Lucy Calkins. He invites his kids to read op-ed pieces/letters to the editor as mentor texts. During writing workshop they discuss the content and form of letters that are most compelling and persuasive. When Chris is confident the students have developed a solid vision of opinion writing by reading like writers, he invites them to take up the practice by composing a letter stating their current position about zoos. Daniel's reflection challenges many status quo positions.

> *Some animals can't do what they would normally do in the wild. For example, elephants would usually, in the wild, run miles a day. But in their enclosures can they run for miles? No! Also when some animals are taken from the wild and get thrown their food they lose their hunting ability. So if the animal were released into the wild it wouldn't know what to do. So the animal eventually dies. That is why I think zoos are bad.*
> —Daniel

As teachers we know we have to close one inquiry to open another. Chris now invites his students to take their opinion/argument and have formal debates with one another; consider and counter diverse perspectives; deepen and broaden their understanding of the topic; and demonstrate their capacity to question, inquire, form opinions, and share and defend those opinions. The edited debate transcript in Figure 3.10 shows how his students have learned these strategies within the context of a student-generated inquiry—one Chris taught into and out of, accomplishing his goals while meeting ELA standards. Chris is teaching children to become informed citizens who are poised to make a critical difference in our democracy.

Debate: Are Zoos Good or Bad?

Derah: Zoos are bad because some animals have small areas to live. Like the koalas, they only have like two trees. And another reason is, in the article, it said that bigger animals like tigers are supposed to have enrichment activities and games. But when we went they were just lying on the ground. And another reason is animals live longer in the wild because animals in the wild can get how much food they want. And another reason is that animals use

---

Figure 3.10 Zoo Debate

continues

their abilities to hunt because when the zoo picks up an animal and then keeps it for a while and raises it, and then drops it back off, the animal thinks that the zookeepers are going to come back and keep feeding it but they're not. And one day it'll probably die. And another reason is that animals have no space, like the green mama, it only had a small area to crawl, but it was a big snake and the tigers have all of that space.

Jenna: Hello, welcome to this debate. Here's a list of how zoos are good. Zoos help populations of animals increase. Zoos used to catch animals from the wild but now they get them from captive breeding programs. Zoos take in animals that are hurt and care for them back to health. Zoos also save some animals from extinction. These are just some of the reasons why zoos are good.

Harlie: A surplus animal is an animal that zoos don't have enough room for. So they either sell them to dealers and other people, which is illegal but they do it anyway. Or they sell them to circuses, like the elephants and the tigers. And so when you go to the circus and you see an elephant and tiger, that's where, I'm guessing, they get them. Or they kill them and feed them to the other animals. That's why I think zoos are bad.

Reese: Zoos really try to—well, why I think zoos are good is because zoos really try to raise the population of the animals close to extinction, like the California condor. It used to—its population used to only be less than 200 and they raised it to around 400.

Harlie: Why I think you're wrong is because if they do that to the animal then they could put some back into the wild. Why don't they put some back into the wild and put some back to the zoo?

Reese: What I think they do is they let the babies drink from their mama and so once they have that milk, they put them back in the wild. And then they feed them the milk.

Hannah: Mine is about how in some zoos, some animals have bigger habitats than others. It's 'cause the bigger their crowd is, the bigger exhibit they have, so that way they can hold more types of those animals. Because most of the times they travel in packs. And the smaller the crowd is, the smaller they are, like when Derah shared that the green mama had a smaller space than the tigers and the lions and the hyenas and all that. If they would just treat the animals the same, there would be nothing to argue about.

Figure 3.10 Zoo Debate, continued

continues

Edwin: Zoos used to get animals straight from the wild but now they use the capital breeding programs to get them easily. Some breeding programs save animals from extinction, like the California condor.

Hannah: Yeah, but sometimes, when their mother doesn't want them, they take them, they get the animals and like Harlie said, they are called surplus animals, and they kill them and feed them to other animals.

Edwin: I think you're wrong about the habitats being smaller sizes because the zoo is too small to have a bunch of big habitats.

Daniel: Why I think zoos are bad is because the animals can't do what they would normally do in the wild. For example, elephants would usually run two miles a day but can they do that in their enclosures? No! I also think that zoos are bad because some animals get captured from the wild, get thrown their food, and are almost forced to have babies. And they eventually lost their hunting ability. So if the animal was released back into the wild, they wouldn't know what to do, and they would eventually die 'cause they would be waiting for the zookeeper who used to have their food. That is why I think zoos are bad.

Patton: I think zoos are good because zoos have improved in 4,000 years and helped raise population levels like the Carolina condor and Père David's deer. And raised $3,000 for a breeding program for animals.

Daniel: I think you're wrong because some animals are still caged up like in the big tunnel in the zoo, they still use those cages except they're coated with glass. And you all know bats are supposed to be in the dark. Well, remember those bats that were in there were in the light.

Patton: It's mostly dark in there, so its dark enough for them to have enough sleep but it's still light enough for us to see them too. So, I don't think that's a problem for the bats.

Calin: I think zoos are bad because some of them are bored in there. They have a really, really short life.

Jack: I think you're wrong because, like, you know in the wild, like, they have, like Daniel said, they have all that space to run around but what if they got hurt and then they were about to get killed because they were getting chased by the type of animal that eats them and then they were most likely to die. But in the zoo, if they were hurt, they can be saved by veterinarians. That's why I think you're wrong.

Figure 3.10 Zoo Debate, continued

continues

Calin: Well, even though there is a veterinarian there, in a zoo you can always get killed easily, very easily.

Jack: Well, zoos are good. Whenever an animal is about to be extinct, they can take a male and a female and breed them with the breeding programs and then they can have babies, and then they can keep some of the babies with other zoos so they can release the mom and dad and the other babies to the wild.

Colby: We have showed y'all that zoos are bad. We have showed that animals are locked up in cages, and some habitats are really small.

Skyler: So you found out why zoos are good. And I will talk about everything you heard. Edwin talked about how though zoos used to get their animals straight from the wild, now they get their animals from recent breeding. Jack says zoos save animals from extinction and he's so very true. Zoos help so many animals from extinction. Patton talked about how zoos have improved greatly in the last 4,000 years. My fact is, when they capture the animal from the wild, they have their enclosure looking ready and looking like their natural habitat so they don't feel too scared or lost. Now remember, zoos are good because of education it gives people and zoos also bring people closer to animals.

Figure 3.10 Zoo Debate, continued

A Critical Investigation of South Carolina's Geography and History *(third-grade unit of study)*

GUIDING QUESTIONS

- Voice: Whose voice is heard or privileged? Whose voice is absent or silenced?
- Power: How might power structures help us better understand this issue?
- Why does the knowledge I'm learning in this unit of study matter in the world?
- Now what? How might we take action on what we have learned during this unit of study?

You can most effectively negotiate the content of the curriculum or standards with kids when deliberately teaching the skillfulness of inquiry. This is easy to do when you teach them to ask critical questions. Just as we don't question the idea that

zoos are wonderful, we typically don't question or critique information in textbooks or curriculum materials. Of course, as educators, we know differently. We know the importance of creating text sets that include primary and secondary sources, and how important it is to ask whose voice is heard and whose voice is missing. We've learned to turn to resources such as Rethinking Schools and The Zinn Education Project for guidance when creating units of study in the social sciences that are truly inclusive.

Tim O'Keefe examines curriculum materials with a critical eye, even when preparing for formal standardized tests. When he and his children encounter surprises or anomalies, they bring them to the center of the conversation and then act on inconsistencies. Surprises inspire them to act, often by writing letters aimed at informing or alleviating injustices. They clarify their understanding and address misconceptions while learning to become thoughtful and engaged citizens in our democracy.

In South Carolina all third graders are expected to learn about the state's people and their history in various regions. Teachers are given consistent information from which to teach. One of the tools that most teachers use, because the content is reflected in the state's annual standardized test, is *South Carolina Studies Weekly: A Weekly Magazine for Young Students of South Carolina.* Because Tim tries to integrate an exploration of the state's history and peoples into his classroom, students approach reading this magazine much like they approach reading and responding to the daily news during morning meeting. They read to learn, to make connections and pose questions about new ideas they encounter.

One day, they noticed a serious miscue, one they suspected was more than an accident, one that reflected a European American rather than Native American perspective.

Tim describes how it all evolved:

We were reading and exploring week 4 together as a class when we noticed some blatantly incorrect information presented in this issue. We had previously studied Native Americans of South Carolina and were aware of the many varied tribes and people among the South Carolina Native Americans. On page 4 of Volume 11, Issue 1, we discovered a graph with false information. The graph, titled "Number of People Living In Colonial South Carolina," obviously did not count the Native Americans among its people. At first we assumed they meant colonists, white European Americans, living in what is now South Carolina, but as we read the corresponding questions, everyone used people, *not* colonists: *"In what year did the most people live in South Carolina? If you add together the number of people in 1670 and 1680, is it greater than or less than the number of people in 1708? If this graph showed the year 1740, do you think there would be more people or fewer people than shown in 1720?"*

Once we recognized the miscue, we talked about it in relation to our guiding questions regarding voice and power. We decided each class member would write a letter to the editors of Social Studies Weekly *magazine asking them to rectify the serious misrepresentation of life in South Carolina for all people. I wrote a letter as well, suggesting they use several graphs or color-code the different populations on the same graph, along with a key, to demonstrate that the dramatic increase of the population of the colonists was directly linked to the steep decline in the population of the native peoples.*

This issue gave me the opportunity to teach children how to speak honestly and respectfully to others in power and to expect change from their actions. And it worked. The children's letters and the email response we received from the magazine's editor-in-chief [see Figure 3.11] *show what is possible when we encourage children to take social action on their learning.*

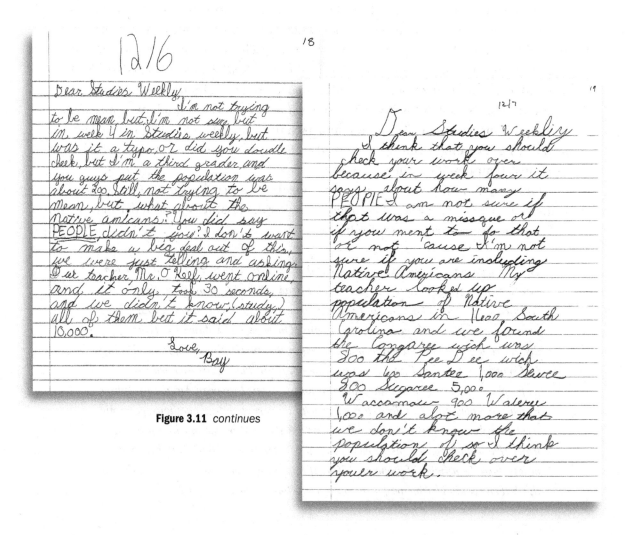

Figure 3.11 *continues*

12/7

Dear Studies Weekly folks,
in week 4 there is a part where
I think is not true, it's when it
said The numbers on this line
graph are rounded to tell you about
how many PEOPLE lived in
South Carolina at diffent times.
And on the graph it said about
200, but I don't think you added
the American Indians and in the
little paragraph that explained the
graph it said how many PEOPLE
that lived in South Carolina, so
I think the about 200 thing
isn't quite right, so if you want to
teach the kids in South Carolina
right you should re-check your
work, so the kids won't grow up
to think that there were only 200
people that lived in South Carolina in 1670
My teacher Mr. O'Keefe went
on the internet and we did some
reseach about Native Americans on
Google we typed in Population Native
Americans in 1600 South Carolina and we got
a Whole lot of information in 1600 their were more

like 10,000 Natives in SC and
their is 15 more that they don't
know what the population is.
I'm not trying to be mean but
200 PEOPLE is not right.
I am sorry that you all ready
published your week 4 Studies
weekly, but I hope you can
make more.
From: Brandon.

Figure 3.11 continued

Email from Editor-in-Chief

Hi, Mr. O'Keefe and students!

Thanks so much for taking the time to write to us about the activity in Week 4. I'm sorry it took a while for me to respond. Our editorial office is in a different place than our main office, and I just received your letters last week.

Our team is in the process of making some updates and revisions to *South Carolina Studies Weekly*, so this was a great time to get the letters. We will look at the activity and make whatever corrections are needed.

Thanks again for sharing your comments with us. We are always glad to hear from students and teachers, as it helps us make our papers the best they can be!

Have a wonderful rest of the school year!

Tim's students learn how their words can change the world. They learn how to write persuasively to people in power, after first reading like writers. They read and discuss editorials, listen to persuasive speeches like National Public Radio's "This I Believe" segments, and talk about how to make positive change effectively and respectively. They grow new identities with a strong sense of agency that will serve them well as students and informed citizens in a democracy.

Make Time and Space for Students to Pose and Investigate Questions in Your Classroom

Whether planning full-blown units of study or mini-inquiries, it helps to shape children's thinking with guiding questions. The questions we ask in life influence what we find, what we see, and what we learn—so, too, in the classroom. We can look at the same text or same experience and glean very different ideas or information from it by simply reframing the questions we ask. Of course, some questions fit particular units of study better than others. It may help to group questions under broad categories for clarity and organization, although many units are served well by questions in a number of categories. Although it's always important to plan with children by soliciting their ideas and questions before and during inquiries, it's essential to have a vision of the kind of thinking you want children to engage in. One of the best ways to help shape children's learning is to teach them how to pose and investigate questions from various perspectives so that they are able to question well.

As you design units of study in the sciences or social sciences, take a look at the questions in Figure 3.2 for inspiration. I hope they will help you consider new possibilities. I've worked with a number of teachers who have found that applying questions like these to units they have taught before transforms the resulting thinking, conversation, and learning. There is nothing sacred about these *particular* questions. They have served me well, and I'm hoping they will do the same for you. They have the potential to broaden and deepen both teaching and learning. I invite you to begin with questions like these in the front rather than the back of your mind, to launch units of study with guiding questions in concert with those your children pose. The questions will prompt you and your students to make careful observations, access primary and secondary sources, use the language of inquiry and of the discipline at hand, and reflect on what you discover.

When you and your students make a habit of looking at the world with questions in mind, the process becomes internalized. You naturally begin generating your own questions with and for your students. It becomes a new way of perceiving the world. Enjoy!

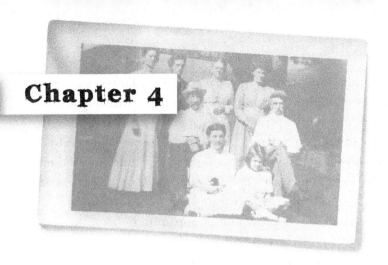

Chapter 4

Strategically Access Primary and Secondary Sources in Complementary Ways

S tudents need to use primary and secondary sources in concert. When historians, anthropologists, biologists, astronomers, and entomologists conduct focused inquiries, they consult secondary sources, but they do so to help them interpret data in and explore questions raised by their primary source investigations. When used together primary and secondary sources complement and extend the learning potential of one another.

Recently, for It's a Grand Day! (CFI's annual whole-school gathering honoring the children's grandparents and significant elders), Tim O'Keefe's second graders shared what they were learning about civil rights by highlighting, through songs, poems, and short biographies, the "heroes of America" who made it possible for us to live and learn together in our beautifully diverse school. After the celebration James Solomon, a charming eighty-year-old, whose grandchild, Carl Lewis, was a student at CFI, spoke to Tim's students about being the first African American to be admitted to graduate school at the University of South Carolina. It was a powerful moment. Instantly, the struggles and triumphs of that tumultuous period in history became real. Everything the students had learned from reading and discussing compelling nonfiction related to civil rights came to life.

Although this was a serendipitous event, CFI teachers plan similar primary source experiences to bring this power to the curriculum regularly. Intentionally creating opportunities for students to encounter primary sources always enhances inquiry. These firsthand encounters can happen in your classroom just as they happen in the bigger world. Chapter 2 features a number of ways wise teachers have inspired children to become careful observers of the world. This chapter builds on those practices by introducing new strategies that bring primary and secondary sources to life in complementary ways. All students deserve these rich opportunities.

Beliefs and Practices Across Grade Levels and Content Areas

When as a profession we began using high-quality nonfiction and historical fiction to complement and extend the limited, often sterile and decontextualized, sometimes inaccurate or outdated information in textbooks, we made tremendous strides. Students in the intermediate grades vicariously experience the tragedy and complexity of the Civil War and come to care about the people affected by it when reading Patricia Polacco's *Pink and Say* (1994). They imagine what life was like for children during World War II when reading Anne Frank's *The Diary of a Young Girl* (1997). They celebrate the heroes of the civil rights movement who worked tirelessly for peace and social justice when reading *Sit-In: How Four Friends Stood Up by Sitting Down* by Andrea Davis Pinkney (2010), *Rosa* by Nikki Giovanni (2007), and *Molly Bannaky* by Alice McGill (2009). The Magic School Bus series (Cole), along with numerous other nonfiction books, enhances students' understanding of space, the water cycle, and plants and animals.

Although adding informational books and magazines to class text sets has enriched our teaching tremendously, they matter more when used alongside primary source observations and investigations. It's fascinating to explore the primary source data available to children through the Internet, firsthand observations, and the people in their lives.

Use Live Webcams to Bring Primary Sources into the Classroom
Kindergarten/first-grade teacher Jennifer Barnes regularly accesses primary sources via live webcams that now capture the natural behavior of animals around the world. Entering a particular animal and its location or region into a search engine and then clicking on the appropriate link brings that animal and its natural environment into

her classroom. When Jennifer's students are looking at the world as ornithologists, they collect data on birds they observe at home and at school; they also witness and analyze the behavior of hummingbirds and eagles via webcams.

To prepare for the all-school field trip to the zoo, Jennifer's students use webcams to practice observing, identifying, and then coding animal behavior together as a class. Jennifer takes them to a pond frequented by flamingos, and they watch for a few moments, noticing and naming the wading birds' behavior. Next, Jennifer has them draw a horizontal and vertical line on a piece of paper or Smart Board and label each quadrant with a behavior (moving the neck, standing on one leg, pecking, etc.). Then each student chooses a flamingo to follow. Every ten seconds Jennifer says, "Stop and code," and these young scientists keep a tally of the behavior of the flamingo they are following. After a couple of minutes they share what they noticed. Jennifer teaches them to be systematic, to verify their tallies with classmates who had followed the same bird, notice patterns, and pose questions about the behavior they have coded.

Then they read about flamingos, reading to learn so that they understand what they had noticed. Jennifer was teaching them the foundational concepts that underlie scientific investigations in the world: validity, reliability, generalizability, and how to use content information to understand and extend knowledge gained through observation.

Jennifer asks her students to take their learning home, assigning homework that directly reflects and extends life in the classroom. The brief excerpts from Jennifer's newsletters, shown in Figure 4.1a, reveal how seamless she makes the transition for both students and their parents. Figure 4.1b shows how Trevor responds to the invitation as a young scientist.

Develop Expert Projects Using Primary and Secondary Sources

Tim O'Keefe used to teach his students about animals, inviting them to become an expert on an animal of their choice. They read, learned to take notes, and then made a presentation on their animal. Tim was successfully teaching his students how to consult nonfiction information and use what they found to teach their friends about their animal. However, his students were not inquiring very deeply and sometimes settled for sharing a few facts.

During a weekly "curricular conversation" (ongoing professional development meeting) Jennifer mentioned how she was using primary and secondary sources in K–1, and Tim immediately transformed his teaching. His newsletter reveals the shift and shows how he has his students take their learning home (see Figure 4.2).

Our inquiry into birds is keeping us busy. We keep finding relevant and important books on birds. And haven't those webcam videos been astonishing? We could not believe all the changes in the nests! Just wait until they tell you the changes we discovered in both nests today! (Check out today's home connection section.)

Talk to your families about the changes in the birds. Can you remember to use the words *fledged* and *solitary?* What about that weather report in Iowa? Hard to believe!

Choose a bird or an animal you can observe in action—an eagle or a humming-bird, a dog or cat, an animal on a zoo webcam, a fish, or even a bee or ant in your yard. Watch the animal a few minutes to ensure you can keep it in sight long enough to observe its behavior. (For flamingos, for example: "puts head down, walks, flaps wings, moves neck." For naked mole rats: "moves backward, crawls frontward, sniffs, digs.")

Chart the behavior using symbols, initials, pictures and/or words. Ask an adult to time you for 2 or 3 minutes, calling out "tally!" every 15 seconds. Scientifically observe and record a tally every 15 seconds under the behavior observed (not what would be fun, cute, or more interesting!). At the end of the time period, look at your data (the tallies under each category). Talk to your parents about what you notice. Which behavior had the greatest number of tallies? The least? Did anything surprising happen during the testing period? **Bring your data chart next Tuesday to share.** (We have done this process in class with flamingoes, penguins, fish, and naked mole rats.)

Figure 4.1a Excerpts from Jennifer's Newsletters

Figure 4.1b Trevor's Response

The World
Is Our Classroom

Dear Parents,

This week we have really gotten into animal observations and expert projects. The very important first step was to select an animal and then to observe it, to learn as much as possible about the animal through direct observations, sketching, and note taking. We learned about our animals' bodies and their behaviors. These observations, learning from the animal itself, are called *primary source information*. Then, the children generated questions about their animals. These questions should, in part, guide their research. Thursday when we went to the computer lab the children did some research about their animals. Everyone left the lab holding some pages printed out from good Internet resources. These *secondary resources* will add to the information they already have through their own observations.

I have demonstrated some procedures for gathering information through primary and secondary resources. We observed night crawlers on two afternoons, sketching and writing detailed notes about their structure as well as their behavior. I took some of my observations and shared them with the children. In my short-hand notes I wrote: *bendy, twisty, can move one part of its body at a time, expand/contract, goes easily in both directions.* From there I wrote some of these notes into an expanded explanation: *I noticed from my observations that worms are very flexible. They can bend and twist in almost any direction! This tells me that worms do not have backbones.*

Here is how I teach note taking: (1) First, read the material. Someone can definitely help you read it if it is too challenging for you to read alone. (2) Then, turn away from the words and pictures and think about what is the most important or most interesting information you want to remember and

Figure 4.2

continues

share. (3) Then, write it down *in your own way, in your own words*. When I asked the children why, they thought it was important to write it "your way," Samantha said, "so that you can really learn it!" I couldn't have said it better. In short, I am coaching the children to **Read * Think *** and ***** **Write It Your Way**. Thursday afternoon many of the children got a good start on this process, and we will take more notes from our secondary resources today. For

next week, we will spend some time each day writing notes. Try to be sure that the children have materials to work with each day. Next week I'll let you know what is expected from the expert projects and when everything is due. For now . . . note taking.

Along with the project presentation (about 5–10 minutes), I am asking that the children write a two-page paper. I am hoping that most of the rough draft will be done in the classroom. What the children write shouldn't sound like the adult author of a book or a scientist. *It should sound like a second-grader.* It should sound like them! Their wonders, observations, and learning should come through. They shouldn't try to make their paper and presentation be like the authors they read. I remember doing my first papers and presentations. I tried to impress my teachers and classmates by throwing in big words I didn't really understand. As Samantha said, this process is important: "So that way you can really learn it!" The children's learning should shine through.

All throughout this process, we have been observing animals and recording notes about their structures and behaviors. At the zoo, we observed penguins. In the classroom, we watched videos of penguins. We watched videos of manatees and recorded notes. Then we read a great little book about them and thought about what we learned through our own observations as well as the book. In the science area we have had many visi-

tors, including tree frog tadpoles, green anole lizards, grasshoppers, crickets, a big toad, and many black swallowtail caterpillars.

Some of the caterpillars came with parsley plants from Woodley's Nursery. Others came from the fennel plants right outside our own classroom window. These have been fascinating to watch. We have observed some from eggs. The tiny larvae are not much larger than this dash (–). But we have been able to

Figure 4.2 continued

continues

watch them eat and eat and grow and grow until they are as big as a child's little finger before they climb up to the top of their enclosure, hang upside down, attach themselves, and molt their skin one final time to reveal the amazing chrysalis beneath.

I have seen this many times and I am always a little breathless at the sight. But the dessert is when we come in one morning and find a swallowtail emerged from its pupa, jet black and velvety, gently pumping its wings back and forth waiting to fly free—and to start the cycle all over again. It is one thing to read about complete metamorphosis from a book, another to watch it on a video. But going outside in the morning to get new fennel, transferring the caterpillars to the fresh green plants, putting down new paper towels in the bottom of the butterfly netting, photographing the growing caterpillars, spotting their shed skins, seeing the two silk strands the larvae use to attach themselves before their final molt, examining the chrysalises at the top of the net, setting the young adult butterflies free . . . *living with the metamorphosis* . . . that is another level entirely. That is living science.

Have a great weekend!

Tim

Figure 4.2 continued

Have Children Conduct Interviews with People Who Matter in Their Lives

Primary sources are as meaningful in the social sciences as they are in the physical, earth, and life sciences. It is incredibly powerful for students to conduct interviews related to artwork, songs, original letters, and so forth, created and composed during a historical period. When students build background knowledge and pose questions based on primary sources, they are more invested in the topic and approach it through an inquiry lens. Their understanding is enriched and deepened.

They Can Learn from Relatives

Students need support when conducting interviews and interpreting artifacts. The CFI first-grade grandparent project gives them that. Students choose the grandparent(s) (someone near and dear to them), conduct an interview, collect and interpret artifacts, and then create a photo essay or memory book. The teachers offer support by having the class generate a list of possible questions to ask. Excerpts from the photo essays shown in Figure 4.3 reveal the teaching and learning potential of this project. The students learn about history through their grandparents' eyes while learning how to gather and report information from a primary source they know and love.

Each first-grade teacher implements the grandparent project her own way; the beauty of teaching through inquiry is that it's generative. Knowing that many children will be spending time with their extended families during this time, Melissa Klosterman launches the project between Thanksgiving and the winter holiday. The students as a class collect data and notice, name, and explore trends. Melissa also weaves questions about grandparents into the fabric of the day (via Venn diagrams on morning sign-in sheets, for example). Students investigate where their grandparents live and create a map representing these locations around the world, from Texas, Pennsylvania, Michigan, West Virginia, North and South Carolina to India and South Korea. They use a timeline to document their grandparents' birthdays. They create a chart of the nicknames they use for their grandparents, i.e., Granddaddy, Nana, Grampie, Grammie, Pawpaw, Gigi, Halmony, Grampie, and Ammama. After the winter break, the first week of the new semester ends with grandparent project presentations at a school-wide celebration on Friday afternoon.

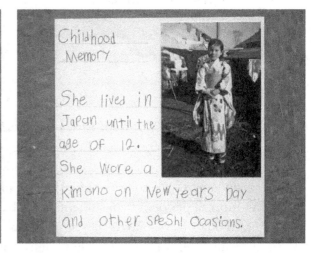

Figure 4.3

They Can Learn About and From Veterans
Tammy Vice invites her fifth graders to consult primary sources to better understand the significance and importance of Veterans Day. She and her students create a list of potential questions to ask, and then students interview a veteran they know and/or invite a veteran to class to be interviewed and honored on Veterans Day. Tears are shed, and funny, delightful stories are told. The parent letter shows how Tammy implements this engagement, and the photos illustrate a couple of their presentations (see Figure 4.4).

Subject: Remembering and Recognizing Our Veterans

Hello Everyone,

Today, our fifth-grade class was discussing what we wanted to do on Thursday in honor of Veterans Day. We decided to highlight veterans that we knew, or knew of, by sharing details about each soldier and his/her military service. We got started by generating a list of guiding questions to help us get basic biographical information. Please feel free to join us in honoring our veterans' service by completing the attached form. Each person in our class will be completing at least one veteran biography, but each of us has the option to do more.

We will be sharing them in class on Thursday morning, starting at 8:30 a.m. We would love for you to visit our classroom during this time. You may just watch or participate by sharing information on a veteran dear to you. If you are unable to make it to our classroom, you may still participate by emailing me your veteran biography or sending it to school with your child.

I know many of our students have family and friends that have served in the armed forces. If you have time, please talk with your child about your or a loved one's military service. If no one close to you has served in the military, having conversations about historical figures or your thoughts about the military are just as important.

Currently, we are studying the Reconstruction Era after the Civil War. However, by the end of the year we will have studied other major wars like World Wars I and II. My hope is for us to connect our learning back to this assignment throughout the year. It will give us a deeper connection to our past through the eyes of those dear to us.

Thank you for your continued support!

Sincerely,
Tammy

Figure 4.4

continues

Directions: Select a veteran, alive or dead, to reflect on. Use the following guidelines to record facts about the individual you have selected. You may choose a family member, neighbor, friend, or historical figure. If you don't know all the facts about the soldier's military service, ask the individual or your parents, or research your historical figure. If you have several veterans in your family that you would like to showcase, please feel free to complete a form for each soldier.

The following information will be filled out using the *veteran's information*.

Name: _____   Rank: _____

Branch of Service: _____   Years of Service: _____
(Examples: USAF, Marines, Army, Navy)
                                                 Age when Enlisted: _____

Outpost or Station: Where did the military send this veteran?
_____
                                                 Circle One: Living or Dead
_____
                                                 Died in Action: Y or N

Did your veteran serve during war or peace time? If during war, what war(s)?

If your soldier died in action, explain how. [OR] Did this soldier suffer injuries during war? If so, what?

Figure 4.4 continued

continues

Did your veteran earn any awards or special honors? If so, what were they?

How did/does your veteran feel or think about his/her military service?

What is your relationship to the veteran you chose to share?

Do you have an artifact from your veteran to share with the class (picture, uniform, award, military memorabilia)?

Figure 4.4 continued

continues

Figure 4.4 continued

Imagine the power of using these interviews as touchstones throughout the year as students learn about World Wars I and II (or any war). The information they encounter will mean so much more because they know and care. We know the value of using touchstone texts when teaching children how to write. We need to expand the notion of touchstones to include learning experiences that get visited and revisited over time to deepen and expand children's learning in the content areas.

Interpret Print-Based Primary Sources

Using historical artifacts as primary sources enhances children's learning (and we now have abundant primary resources at our fingertips via the Internet). Fourth- and fifth-grade teacher Julie Waugh puts it this way: "Historical primary resources can be a great introduction to a historical event. Giving students a primary source to interpret about which they have no background knowledge creates a 'need to know.' Students are ripe for using other resources (primary and secondary) to find out more. Introducing primary sources after students have a wealth of information about a historical event is an excellent assessment tool. It helps you discover whether students can use and apply what they have used to a new situation."

Before teaching her students about the Boston Tea Party, Julie has them read original letters written during the time period. They are intrigued, generating hypotheses and posing questions. They debate what might be happening and why. Once they are hooked, Julie reveals the incident and directs them to secondary sources in which they can explore their questions and hunches. The guiding questions in Figure 4.5 help students interpret historical artifacts.

Good Questions to Use with Print-Based Primary Documents:

- Who is the audience for this document? What evidence do you have?
- What is the purpose of this document? Why was it created?
- What do you know?
- What questions do you have?
- When was this document created?
- Whose voice is represented in the document? Whose voice is missing?

For Letters:

- Who wrote this letter?
- When?
- To whom did they write it?
- Why was this letter written? How do you know?
- What do you know?
- What questions do you have?

Figure 4.5

Make Time and Space for Students to Access Primary and Secondary Sources in Your Classroom

For the most part, current curriculum materials include abundant secondary sources. Teachers regularly use picture books and chapter books to complement and extend curriculum materials designed to teach science and social studies. The primary source opportunities are what make learning in school as authentic as learning in the larger world. As you envision the units you plan to teach, ask yourself questions like:

- Who encounters or investigates problems like this?
- What data do they use?
- How do they do their work?
- How might these primary sources (data or people) help your students make careful observations, inspire their questions, and/or serve as an audience for their opinion or persuasive writing?

Although there are tremendous challenges in teaching these days, technology makes it possible to access primary sources virtually—whether we want to witness changes in the earth's surface over time, track the impact of global warming on plant and animal life, or view a civil rights leader in action in the 1960s.

Think first about live demonstrations from primary sources; they are the most memorable and informative touchstones. When you are unable to arrange firsthand visits, there is a very good chance that you will find primary sources (documents or artifacts from the period or interviews with people who have lived through the experience) via the Internet.

You may want to launch an inquiry with an investigation into a primary source at some point; doing so will inspire your students to wonder and discover before they read to learn. Other times you will want your students to read, write, and talk their way into understanding an issue or topic before introducing a primary source. The more they know, the more sophisticated their questions become.

Once students "read around" for a bit and write about what they've read, you can invite them to document what they have learned and what they want to know now. The point is to help them read, write, think, and talk as inquirers—to help them recognize how strategic learners construct knowledge in the world using both primary and secondary sources.

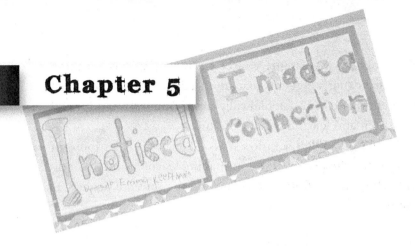

Chapter 5

Use the Language of Inquiry to Learn and Communicate New Understanding

Listen as teachers and children engage in talk that matters—talk that promotes new connections and deep, lasting understanding and generates new learning:

"I wonder . . ."

"I was surprised by . . ."

"I have a hunch why Pluto was demoted as a planet."

"Building on Jevon's idea . . ."

"I'm thinking . . ."

"Connecting to Madeline's question . . ."

"That's a strategy mathematicians often use."

"Why do you think that?"

"What inspired you to write this piece?"

"Does this remind you of other books we've read together?"

"Now that we have learned so much about the civil rights movement, what new questions do you have?"

Long ago Vygotsky (1978) taught us that language directs as well as reflects our thinking. In response, we plan learning engagements that are social, not simply individual, cognitive processes. We intentionally and systematically create opportunities for children to work together, to teach and learn from one another.

More recently, Judith Lindfors (1999), Gordon Wells (1986), and Peter Johnston (2004, 2012) have demonstrated the power of talk in shaping learners and learning. We now see how talk influences the identities we create and the sense of agency (or lack thereof) that we embrace.

Talk Always Matters, in All Schools

Educators who visit the Center for Inquiry consistently marvel at the nature of the talk that permeates our classrooms, from kindergarten through fifth grade. Here is what they have noticed.

- The language used with all learners, tall and small, is consistent.
- Teacher talk shows a genuine respect for children's capacity to construct and share knowledge.
- Our teachers "think up" with children rather than talk down to them.
- Teachers and students move fluidly in and out of mentor and apprentice roles as they talk their way into understanding.
- Children at all grade levels can talk about what they are doing and why.
- Students are as likely to turn to one another as to their teacher when confronted with an anomaly or challenge.
- Teachers and students create curriculum together through reflective conversations and strategy-sharing sessions.
- Students use the language of inquiry as naturally as their teachers do; it permeates our culture.

Recently, visiting teachers and administrators from Manitoba made a number of connections and posed thoughtful questions throughout their visit. After they returned home, a leader of the group sent the following email that illuminates the symbiotic nature of talk and inquiry.

Hello Heidi,

Greetings from Winnipeg! We all arrived safe and sound back home without any delays from snowstorms (much to our sadness). Many of us hoped we'd be stranded in South Carolina so that we could spend another day at the Center. What an amazing day we had!

As you know, we're all at very different spots in terms of our understanding of inquiry, so the experience was different for each of us. For some, it was eye-opening to see young children engaged in such authentic learning, using sophisticated language and thinking processes. For others, it was a chance to reaffirm our own personal beliefs and see those beliefs in practice throughout an entire school. We left the Center feeling energized and hopeful.

Since our visit, we've been deeply engaged in conversations around:

- *providing authentic learning experiences for kids in our classrooms*
- *creating a culture of trust and love in our classrooms (and in our whole school)*
- *the language of inquiry that was woven into all of your classrooms*
- *the notion of "thinking up" with children and colleagues*
- *the challenge of providing support to children who don't have support from home, as well as finding ways to increase parental engagement.*

A heartfelt thank-you for the time you gave us last week—for making us think deeply, for opening your classrooms to us, for sharing your children with us, for making us feel so welcome. Thank you. Thank you. Thank you.

These teachers noticed that talk matters at the Center for Inquiry. They are right; it does. However, talk *always* matters in *all* classrooms. It always has and always will. I have the privilege of also working extensively with the faculty of the Greenwood School of Inquiry (GSI) in South Carolina. I'm helping them generate new beliefs around inquiry-based practices throughout their school. As they have reflected on the first two years of their journey, they believe that it is the talk—embracing the language of inquiry—that has been the most transformative. By intentionally using the language of inquiry and foregrounding the authentic vocabulary used in the various disciplines, these remarkable teachers have created a culture of inquiry within their classrooms and throughout the school.

At the Center for Inquiry, it all began during one of our weekly curricular conversations as we were watching a video clip of Tim O'Keefe interacting with his third graders. They were learning to work as botanists, and we were inspired by the nature of Tim's talk with his students. Because other teachers longed for their rooms to sound like his, we watched several videos from Tim's second- and third-grade classrooms, and we identified the verbal stems he and his students used most frequently and the conversational moves they made. We created a list of prompts to guide our talk (see Figure 5.1). This list made an immediate difference within individual classrooms and throughout the school, and it has become a powerful tool for new faculty and teaching interns alike. When teachers begin talking the talk, it is only a matter of days before children begin following their lead. Once the children internalize the talk, their thinking and interaction patterns are reshaped, and they experience a new way of being.

Talk That Promotes Inquiry:

I noticed . . .

I wondered . . .

I appreciated . . .

I learned . . .

I felt . . .

I thought . . .

I made a connection . . .

Talk That Promotes Genuine Conversation:

Help me understand your idea . . .

Why do you think that?

Building on _____'s comment . . .

I have a connection to _____'s response.

Where did you find that idea in the text?

I was surprised by _____'s perspective.

This reminds me of other [books, authors, experiences, learning engagements, etc.].

Figure 5.1

Beliefs and Practices Across Grade Levels and Content Areas

Make Language Visible and Accessible

Although all of our teachers intentionally use the language of inquiry and see that their children do so as well, many have found it helpful to post the language in their classrooms. Melissa Klosterman invites her students to create posters at the beginning of the year, which she then puts in places of honor in her classroom (see Figure 5.2). These lists and posters become touchstones for talk and promote productive talk throughout the year.

Figure 5.2

Talk Reader-to-Reader, Writer-to-Writer, Mathematician-to-Mathematician, Scientist-to-Scientist, and Social Scientist-to-Social Scientist

If we want learning in school to reflect the way readers, writers, mathematicians, scientists, and social scientists live, learn, and communicate in the world, one of the most effective and efficient shifts we can make is how we talk to and with our students. When we talk scientist-to-scientist, mathematician-to-mathematician, writer-to-writer (in lieu of teacher-to-student), we weave the vocabulary of the discipline into the conversation and illustrate how to talk our way into understanding. This often begins with teachers' noticing and naming the kind of stance within the discipline that children are implicitly using, such as "That's the kind of question a mathematician might ask" or "You are looking at that artifact like an archeologist." By being mindful of this stance, teachers help shape children's identities. They send messages that their students are already demonstrating their capacity to think and wonder across disciplines. Michelle Kimpson illustrates this stance in her morning message. She and her K–1 teaching colleagues make a habit of naming the lens—the discipline or profession—children are using to explore the world at different points in the year. When they are

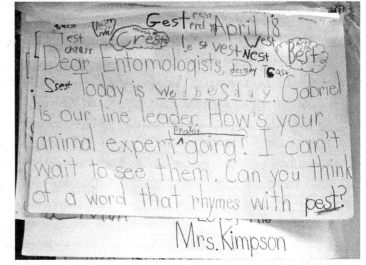

Figure 5.3

studying insects, she refers to them as *entomologists* (see Figure 5.3); when they are studying space, she refers to them as *astronomers;* and so on. She does so in talk and in print.

When Jennifer Barnes creates templates to guide her students' thinking during scientific investigations, she sends the message that they are working as scientists while introducing and reinforcing the language that scientists use (see Figure 5.4).

Weave the Language of the Disciplines into Talk and Print

Every form of communication—writing, mathematics, art, music, movement—conveys meaning in uniquely compelling ways. That's why they exist; we wouldn't need

Figure 5.4

them if they didn't offer something special. As humans we've invented sign systems that best convey specific emotions, ideas, or questions. The old adage "a picture is worth a thousand words" beautifully expresses this notion.

As teachers, we can release the communication potential in our classrooms by encouraging children to construct and share meaning across sign systems. We can also help them use each sign system powerfully by exploring the language of inquiry, as played out by authors, mathematicians, artists, musicians, and dancers. Susanne Pender is intentional about teaching children the unique language of the disciplines. She uses her classroom walls as teaching tools, reminders of what they've learned about how to communicate across disciplines (see Figure 5.5).

The pictures shown in Figure 5.5 illustrate how important and challenging it is to use precise language as mathematicians while also communicating that math is a tool for learning and understanding our world.

Susanne's teaching walls "speak" to us. "Reading" them reveals the content, vocabulary, and processes of the discipline her students are learning together (see Figure 5.6).

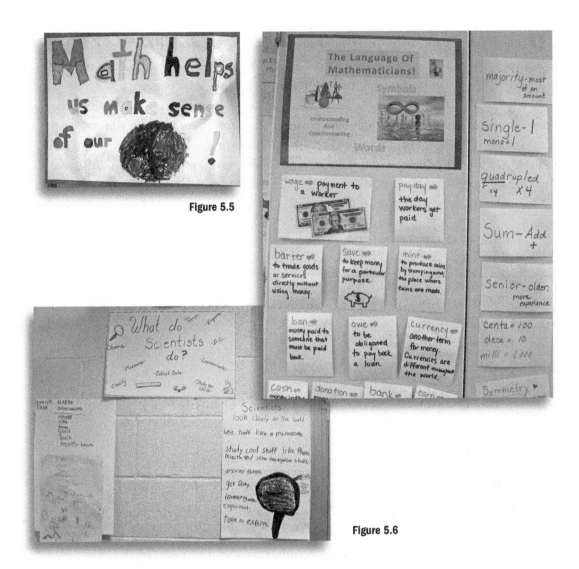

Figure 5.5

Figure 5.6

Promote the Skillfulness of Inquiry

Inquiry is the driving force in all curricular structures and all formal units of study. It reflects how knowledge is constructed and shared in the world. For students to develop habits that will serve them well into the next century, they need intense, broad-based opportunities during reading and writing workshop to discover well-crafted language and effective strategies for constructing and sharing meaning; during math workshop to investigate the skills and strategies that mathematicians have devised to carry out their investigations; and during integrated units of study to delve into ways of using reading, writing, and math as tools for learning. We intentionally and systematically teach the skillfulness of inquiry—*how* to learn—while simultaneously teaching *what* to learn.

Teach Students to Think and Communicate Across Disciplines

Second-grade teacher Brandon Foote recognizes the importance of teaching children how to think, learn, and communicate across disciplines. Making space for what he values most in the curriculum, he launches the year with an inquiry into the disciplines themselves. He and his children engage in mini-inquiries to understand the purposes, processes, language, and tools used across the disciplines. They begin with guiding questions in mind, which follow. These questions reveal the standards that they will address together throughout the year, and that Brandon knows will give his teaching a lift once children understand their value.

GUIDING QUESTIONS

Math

- In what ways is math used around us?
- How many different ways can we find numbers being used?
- What are different ways of counting?
- How do mathematicians talk about their work?
- What questions do mathematicians ask?
- What do math symbols represent?
- How do mathematicians come to understand symbols?

Writing

- Why write?
- What is the authoring cycle?
- How does a writer use a writer's notebook?
- How do writers capture experiences through their words?
- How do we talk about our writing?
- How do writers make their pieces interesting and meaningful?
- What questions do writers ask?

Reading

- What is reading?
- What strategies do readers use to figure out unfamiliar words? To make meaning?
- How do readers choose just-right books?
- How do readers approach fiction and nonfiction?
- In what ways do readers respond to what they have read?
- How do readers communicate?
- In what ways can reading help our writing?

Social Studies

- What is a community?
- How do we live as a community?
- How do our communities influence our classroom community?
- What strategies are used to read a map?
- How do social scientists talk about the world?
- How do people make a difference or bring about change? What tools do they use?
- How can numbers help us make sense of our community?
- By looking closely, can we notice change?

Science

- What tools do scientists use? What is the purpose of these tools?
- What types of science do we use each day?
- What do scientists do?
- How do scientists talk about their work?
- How do plants and animals impact community?
- How do animals and plants change?
- How are the major classifications of animals similar? How are they different?
- How do people change the natural community?
- How is energy passed through organisms?

By doing this, Brandon takes the first few weeks of school to inquire into—to talk about—the ways readers, writers, mathematicians, scientists, and social scientists construct and share knowledge in the world. His goal is to have learning in school more closely parallel authentic, rigorous learning in the larger world. Brandon's intent comes to life as he describes his plans:

> *The nature of this unit requires understanding how inquirers learn, think, and communicate. Therefore, it will be wide-ranging in its methodology. Observations will be done in a variety of contexts and environments, experiments will be done in class and at home, surveys will be conducted on various topics and questions, families will be interviewed, etc. The goal is to analyze these subjects from various perspectives: a sociologist might be interested in geography to see how people change locations over time, a mathematician may be interested in the same topic because he or she would like to see patterns in population increase or decrease, a man interested in his family history might want to know where his ancestors lived, etc. We don't*

have to rely on only one method to approach subjects, topics, or questions. As we move through this year, my hope is that we see much diversity in the ideas students bring to the table.

By taking the time to explore both the language of inquiry and the tools used across disciplines within the context of this first unit of study, Brandon creates touchstones in each content area. He will refer to these touchstones during second and third grade as he shows his students how to learn about and through the disciplines.

Teach the Language of the Disciplines Through Discussion of Authentic Texts

Many early childhood teachers introduce their students to weather using commercial products designed to "teach" the basics. You know the materials I'm talking about, things like cute pictures of the sun and clouds; they haven't changed much over the past fifty years.

To bring authenticity to her weather unit, K–1 teacher Michelle Kimpson collects a series of weather sections from the local newspaper and uses them to teach children the vocabulary, symbols, and function of meteorology. She leads conversations around these real-world texts during science workshop, launching them by reminding students to look at the date, as well as other features, to help them understand what was happening meteorologically in various places at that time. Next, Michelle makes a connection to their previous conversations about weather by suggesting that they look for wind patterns. Then she ponders, "I wonder if we might learn anything about the three main kinds of clouds we've been exploring? Let's think together to remember."

Ross offers, "Cirrus!"

Megan adds, "Stratus."

Kennedy contributes, "Cumulus clouds!"

Michelle reminds them that we often see different combinations of these clouds and then asks, "What else might we find?"

"Temperatures!"

Michelle leads them to make personal connections with content information. "Yes, you might even look to see whether you can find temperatures in faraway places like China. Yesterday we found out that the weather in the part of China where Joyce's family is from was close to our temperature here. We looked at Canada because Megan's mom is from Canada and Texas because Ms. Portland is from Texas."

When Hunter notices that the weather pages tell about lake levels and tides in South Carolina, Michelle asks a very important question, one that helps kids recognize the significance of their learning: "Who would like to know this information?"

Hunter responds, "If you want to go on a boat. And my dad is in Myrtle Beach, so he might want to check on high and low tides."

Michelle now sends the kids off in pairs to notice, name, and share what they find most interesting when reading the weather section of the paper (see Figure 5.7). After about fifteen minutes of exploratory conversation, they form a circle to reflect on what they've noticed. Michelle again carefully orchestrates how to learn vocabulary and content using the newspaper and kids' observations and questions as her primary teaching tools. Together they explore:

- climate
- temperature
- the relationship between the date, temperature, and location
- regional, state, national, and international temperatures and why it's useful to know this information
- trends or patterns in the daily temperature and climate for the state of South Carolina.

Figure 5.7

Not bad for first graders! They are becoming sophisticated consumers of newsprint, developing a conceptual understanding of weather and using the language of meteorologists and climatologists.

Honor Children's Everyday Language and Use It as a Scaffold to Academic Language

We all remember how children learn to talk, and we celebrate their approximations while they are doing so. We are comfortable fostering the development of oral language by immersing children in ongoing conversations and providing intentional demonstrations of words in context. Unfortunately, though, as soon as children cross the threshold of elementary school, we feel such pressure to move them forward that we often forget the importance of honoring children's everyday language while bringing them into the fold of academic language.

K–1 teacher Susan Bolte reminds us to build on the language children bring to the classroom. When teaching her students to make observations as geologists, Susan begins by capturing the words her young geologists use to describe rocks and their formations during class experiments. She speaks to them as budding geologists and weaves the language geologists use into her talk while celebrating the words they use as they acclimate themselves to this new way of viewing and describing the world (see Figure 5.8).

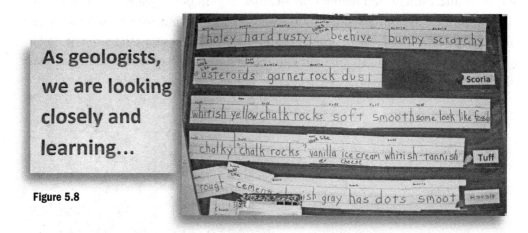

As geologists, we are looking closely and learning...

Figure 5.8

Susan's geology workshop is filled with the sights and sounds of young geologists talking their way into understanding, much like adults who are learning something new in the company of others. Susan provides daily demonstrations. She also uses nonfiction big books and read-alouds to explicitly teach her students the content and language of geology. However, it's the intimacy of her side-by-side work with students that inspires deep learning. She carefully tracks their thinking and makes connections between their shared learning history and their current experience.

When Susan invites her young geologists to assess the composition of rocks using the Mohs hardness test, she works alongside them and takes dictation, documenting their oral language and using it to intuit their current understanding. Simultaneously, she builds on their talk to make connections between their words and those that geologists use to describe the phenomena.

- "Yes, it is a lot like sand. Geologists named those rocks *tuff*. And petrologists have studied where rocks come from. This kind of rock, tuff, comes from volcanic ash."
- "You are noticing that some rocks are harder than others. That's why geologists created the hardness test, to see which rocks are hardest and which ones are softest."
- "Great connection! Your descriptions match those that geologists make. Do you remember the book we shared a few days ago that told us about the three rock types, igneous, sedimentary, and metamorphic?"

Susan has a vision of the content and processes she wants her young geologists to learn and brings that vision to life through rich conversations. She carefully scaffolds children's understanding by making connections among the known, their everyday language, and the language geologists and petrologists use to describe our world.

Make the Language of Inquiry and of the Disciplines Central to Your Classroom Talk

As you listen to and analyze the talk in your classroom or school, remember that it is challenging to isolate the parts from the whole. A hologram seems to be the best model for conveying our beliefs about talk: Even though you might focus on a particular dimension of talk to hone your teaching, every part is central to the whole and the whole is in each part.

During a five-minute conversation about mathematics, for example, you might notice and name strategies children are employing to talk mathematician-to-mathematician. At the same time, you will likely pose questions to encourage children to act on the data they've collected and analyzed and help them think of ways to do so. Noticing and naming are inexplicably part of the whole.

Talk is always contextualized. You and your students may occasionally examine talk as a way to develop community, but for the most part you scaffold children's talk during authentic learning engagements. Just as it's not enough to talk about building community, it's not enough to talk about talk. The most powerful talk takes you and your students to new places—it promotes understanding (of content, strategies, relationships). As part of compelling and effective learning, talk:

- fosters and reflects the ways passionate, accomplished practitioners of the discipline live, learn, and communicate in the world
- promotes knowledge construction rather than transmission
- helps children grasp and use the unique language of the discipline
- promotes skillful inquiry
- leads to reflection and reflexivity
- builds a strong identity as a practitioner of the discipline
- promotes agency and social action.

There are many ways to improve talk in the classroom. Begin by posting the common prompts and conversational strategies in Figure 5.1 on your wall, inscribing them on bookmarks, or asking children to enter them in their notebooks. Used during small-group or whole-group conversations, they soon become a habit—and an integral part of the classroom or school culture.

Historically we have frontloaded vocabulary. We've attempted to teach it before students read or encounter it in a learning experience. For this reason, intentionally weaving the language of various disciplines into the fabric of your conversations may seem counterintuitive, but doing so improves the quality of those conversations immeasurably. Instruction makes the most sense to children when you weave new vocabulary into authentic learning experiences, highlight it in context, and build bridges between the language children use and that used by various academic disciplines. Remembering how children learn oral language outside school will help you teach in ways that are congruent with the learning process.

You also need to create text sets of *real* books, magazines, and newspapers, printed and virtual. Too often textbooks contain sterile, decontextualized information. The language of inquiry and of the disciplines lives in authentic publications. If the texts are too sophisticated for children to read independently, read them aloud or invite students to read the pictures, models, graphs, maps, and captions. You will be teaching foundational strategies for navigating nonfiction texts while teaching them the vocabulary of the discipline.

Chapter 6

Use Reflection and Self-Evaluation to Grow and Change

Reflection matters. It's the process that holds all the other processes together and helps us move forward by looking back. Even though tons of books and articles have been written on the importance of reflection, the teachers at the Center for Inquiry initially underestimated its role. But now that we understand its significance for learners, we weave reflective engagements into the fabric of our curriculum.

We create conditions for children to reflect on their learning in all classrooms, as part of curricular structures, day in and day out. Reflective talk takes place during intimate conferences as well as whole-class, strategy-sharing sessions. Students pause and attend to their friends' ideas or strategies during a workshop. Teachers formally recognize and celebrate an effective strategy used by a child or small group and suggest that others may want to try it out. They guide children's reflective thinking during individual or small-group conferences. They build strategy sharing into the workshop framework to ensure children have ongoing opportunities to reflect on and share their learning.

Routines and rituals are important inside and outside of school. It's extremely helpful to use a consistent structure in workshops in all disciplines, because teachers and children thrive in predictable learning environments. It's comforting to know what to expect. Therefore, we embrace a workshop model with the following components, which correspond with how learning works in the world.

- *Demonstration:* Teachers use strategy lessons or minilessons to show students how to use an idea or strategy and why it makes a difference.
- *Engagement:* Students live the process by reading, writing, engaging in mathematical investigations, working on an experiment, interpreting an artifact, and so on.
- *Reflection:* Individuals, groups, or the whole class think about and evaluate the content, skills, strategies, or concepts explored during the engagement phase.
- *Celebration:* Teachers and students formally and informally recognize growth and change.

Teachers and kids know they can count on these regular opportunities for students to be shown how to do something, try it out for themselves, reflect on what worked and what didn't, and celebrate their accomplishments.

Making reflection part of instruction also promotes authentic accountability. When kids know they will have an opportunity to reflect on and share something significant they learn or try during workshop, they are more invested and intentional when working independently. They take learning seriously, knowing that their teacher and friends are counting on them to offer thoughtful advice or ideas. When children talk about their struggles, their questions, the strategies that work, they become more familiar with and control the process. Going public with their strategies, children become essential mentors for their classmates and their teachers. Individual insights become part of the collective learning. We create the conditions for collaborative inquiry when we bring the sage wisdom of the Native American Siletz tribe to life: "One who learns from one who is learning drinks from a running stream."

Like most shifts in pedagogy, this is often easier said than done in the beginning. Teachers often find themselves doing all the work, all the thinking, all the reflecting. And accomplished, effective teachers do work hard and reflect constantly. However, since genuine learning takes place through firsthand engagement with and reflection on the content and processes being used, it is accomplished best as a collaborative venture (see Figure 6.1). When we invite kids to join

Knowing and Being Known

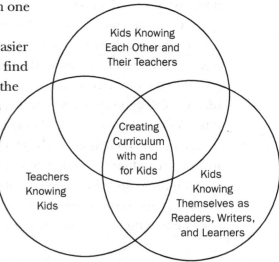

Figure 6.1

us in working intensively and extensively, reflecting regularly, and setting new goals by which to grow and change, everyone benefits.

Beliefs and Practices Across Grade Levels and Content Areas

In this approach to teaching and learning, teachers make and document careful observations of their students as learners. They then explicitly teach the skills and strategies related to inquiry by sharing their own work as readers, writers, mathematicians, scientists, and social scientists (during the demonstration phase of the workshop) while also making space in the curriculum for children to do so with one another (during the engagement phase). Additionally, teachers create learning experiences during the reflection phase that help students get in touch with themselves as learners and with the learning process. When these three dimensions come together, individual and collective learning is enhanced. In the examples that follow you will see how teachers weave reflection into the fabric of the curriculum. You will see how reflection promotes the co-construction of knowledge. Reflection serves as the impetus for individual and collective growth and change. You will see how reflection matters across the curriculum and grade levels. It holds everything and everyone together while promoting and sustaining joyful rigor.

Make Reflection a Habit of the Heart and Mind

From the first day of kindergarten, when children form a friendship circle to share something they learned before heading home, to fifth-grade graduation, when teachers publicly reflect on the unique strengths, insights, and stories each child brought to the school community, kids and teachers at the Center for Inquiry reflect.

Kindergartners comment on the books they are reading independently or with friends: the bilateral symmetry of a butterfly, patterns in their Lego constructions, strategies for counting efficiently, something surprising in the attendance graph, wondrous words they heard and then posted on the word wall, books they are writing, nature pictures they are taking, sketches of their science experiments, and so on.

Teachers highlight an interesting craft move made by a young author or the way a small group decided to try a challenging math strategy to solve a problem. They also celebrate lessons learned through mistakes or miscues, sending the important message that learning does not mean getting every word, problem, or experiment right the first time. They teach responsively, reflecting publicly on children's learning and then making new instructional decisions based on what they notice.

At fifth-grade graduation, students' unique academic identities and contributions to their classroom community are acknowledged. When my son Colin graduated, his teacher, Brent Petersen, remarked:

Your friends know you as a human calculator. You can double numbers faster than most of us can count. You are a true friend, and I am sure I have never seen students fight over a partner like they do for you. You are funny, caring, and a true learner. I appreciate you for the kindness and compassion you possess. You are always insightful and sincere, and your ideas always seem to come out like quotes from an ancient theologian. You have made such an impression on so many here at the Center. You have made fourth and fifth grade wonderful for me to teach. And it was pretty fun rolling you down the hill at Earthshine! The face of the Center will change without you here, Colin O'Keefe.

Imagine what it is like for each and every child to be celebrated in this way before moving on to middle school. It's a powerful rite of passage.

Share Strategies

Five- to ten-minute sharing sessions at the end of a workshop make children aware of their own learning, and these are rich opportunities for students to move in and out of mentor and apprentice roles. The process is the same whether kids are sharing efficient reading strategies, surprising new insights about Native Americans, compelling questions about the origin of the universe, or effective strategies used during mathematical investigations. The common purpose, whatever the content area or grade level, is to reflect on and share insights and strategies. Individual ideas then become part of the class's collective learning.

Because we want our students to learn to think, work, and communicate as mathematicians, we invite them to learn math concepts as well as algorithms. Tim O'Keefe leads an inquiry into measurement with nonstandard units (an inquiry originally developed by David Whitin and described in Mills, O'Keefe, and Whitin 1996) by reading *How Big Is a Foot?* by Rolf Myller (1991), a delightful story illustrating how humans use nonstandard units of measurement while pointing to the importance of standard units of measurement.

Tim then invites his students to think and talk about the conflict that emerges in the story. The king and the apprentice have feet that are different lengths. The importance of standard units of measurement is implied, but Tim wants his students to see this—to truly understand it—for themselves. So, he has pairs of students measure a variety of items in the room using nonstandard units of measure (see Figure 6.2).

After about fifteen minutes, they reconvene for a reflective strategy-sharing session.

Notice and Name Students' Strategies

Tim opens the reflection by referring to his "kid-watching" clipboard and telling the students what he has noticed while the kids were working:

"You solved problems in an interesting way, much like mathematicians do. You may not always use the same language that mathematicians do, but you solved problems like they do. You created your own ways of doing things. For example, if something couldn't be measured by an exact number of a particular unit, lots of kids mixed units. That's what we all do when we measure things. If we were going to measure my height, most people would say I'm five feet eleven inches. We would use two units, the big unit until it won't fit anymore and then smaller units. I noticed a lot of kids doing things like that. Chelxyn used two palms and two digits when he was measuring something. Jeremy used fingernails and knuckles. Katie measured Amber and said she was two fathoms, two palms, and one finger. So that's what we do. We start with the bigger units, and when we have leftover space we use smaller and smaller units. That's what mathematicians do. It was really nice to see you guys doing that. I also noticed some of you talking mathematics. Zachary was saying he was using mixed numbers, which of course are whole numbers and parts of numbers. Many of you were using small units that you made up, like Jeremy was using fingertips and fingernails."

Then Tim opens the floor to the children, calling on Margaret. She says, "One of the things I did was measure Elizabeth. She was ten palms. Elizabeth did [measured] me and she said I was one fathom."

Paxie chimes in, "When I was measuring Katie, I think she was about one fathom."

Katie says, "Well, when I was measuring McKay I first measured her with my feet by walking around her on the floor. Then I measured her with my fingers and then I measured her with a fathom. So I measured her in three different ways."

Jonathon contributes, "When I was measuring the big pillow I figured out that Kenan measured it with cubits and I measured it with a yard, and then I figured out a yard was two cubits."

Non-Standard Units of Measure

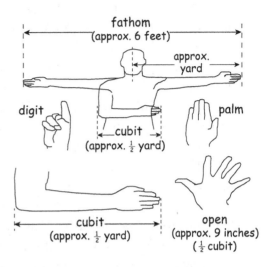

Figure 6.2

Zach is bursting with excitement to add to the conversation. "I noticed it depends on how long your arms are to have a complete fathom. Because if we use Mr. O'Keefe's arms on Jonathon for a fathom then they would be taller than Jonathon. But if we used my arms it would be his exact height."

Zach's comment beautifully fulfills the learning potential of this experience. Tim thanks Zach for his insight and uses it as an example of why standard units of measurement are necessary to communicate precise measurements. He tells the class they will build on this experience in the next few days with projects using standard units of measurement.

Throughout this conversation Tim talks to his students mathematician-to-mathematician, explicitly connecting their work and language with the strategies mathematicians use. As the children share what they have done and what they have noticed, they connect events of the story and their personal nonstandard measurement experiences with the emergence of standard units of measurement. Their learning increases individually and collectively because they have the chance to reflect.

Set Goals and Reflect on Successes and Challenges (expert projects)

Students make learning their own by showcasing a special expertise or talent. CFI kindergartners' first presentation is a "personal passion project" on a topic they already know a great deal about, something they love and would like to teach their friends. They share everything from feeding a baby to cheerleading to shell collecting to horseback riding. It's also a way for their teachers to get to know their students in new ways. Their topics reveal so much about who they are both as people and as learners.

Teachers teach the process—how to learn and how to show what you know. They scaffold their instruction carefully, helping students use photos, demonstrations, sketches, labels, or focused text in their own language and spelling. Teachers also complete their own expert project to demonstrate the process. Parents are explicitly told, in newsletters and on curriculum night, that they are to support their children—not to direct, control, or do the project for them. We want children to experience the delight of being given the chance to shine, to show what they know. Personal passion projects help the children and teachers get to know one another. They help students learn how to build on what they already know by reading about it, talking with others, and then sharing it with their friends in writing, as a sketch, or doing a demonstration (see Figure 6.3).

Figure 6.3

Offer Feedback: Three Pluses and a Wish

Children complete their presentations by saying, "I'm ready for questions or comments." They then receive immediate oral feedback from their teacher (see the form in Figure 6.4) and appreciations and wonderings from their friends.

Expert Project

Expert's Name _____ Topic _____ Date _____

+

+

+

Wish:

Goal:

(Mills and Donnelly 2001)

Figure 6.4

Michelle Kimpson and her colleagues videotape their kindergartners' expert project presentations so parents can share the experience without having to leave home or work. (Often, these videos become family treasures.) They invite parents to complete the "three pluses and a wish" form as well. Children celebrate their accomplishments, consider next steps, and set new goals with feedback from their teacher, parents, and classmates. Before students begin their next expert project, teachers remind them to focus on their individual and collective goals.

Brandon Foote uses expert projects to personalize social studies. To help his students understand and appreciate diverse cultures or ways of being in the world, he invites them to select a country they are especially connected to in some way. After researching their country, the children document their new learning by completing and presenting an expert project.

Brandon sees tremendous benefits in designing expert projects around required standards:

> We look at how governments and economies of these countries are run, how cultures affect life there, and how the countries are similar to or different from our own country. Some would argue that a whole-class unit on a particular country would accomplish similar goals and also cover multiple standards; however, the major difference between a whole-class unit on a particular country and these individual expert projects driven by interest or passion is where the knowledge originates. With expert projects, students not only acquire knowledge but also, by listening and responding to others, begin to view one another as trustworthy sources of information with the authority and know-how to communicate their findings clearly to an audience.

Expert projects promote and reflect growth. We want kids to become experts as readers, writers, mathematicians, scientists, and social scientists. Of course we want them to learn material required by curricular standards. But we want more. We want them to connect the information or strategies to their lives. Expert projects do that. After kids learn foundational knowledge during a unit of study, they begin their own inquiries within the larger unit. They begin developing personal expertise.

Become an Expert on a Favorite Author

Expert projects are not limited to science or social studies topics. To help our kindergartners get in touch with themselves as readers before they return as first graders, we ask them to find an author they love and read as many books as they can by that author during the summer between kindergarten and first grade. From the first day of kindergarten their teachers have asked them what they notice during read-alouds and shared reading, and they have named these things on classroom charts. So by this time the students are primed to notice craft techniques and an author's unique voice and style.

Thus, they are ready to embark on an author study early in first grade. They first become "author experts" as a class. One year a class chose Leo Lionni. As they inquired about him as a writer, they learned to read like writers. As they named the moves he made as an author, their teacher Jennifer Barnes documented these moves on classroom charts and in newsletters, and then the children tried these moves for themselves. Jennifer uses her parent newsletter to encourage parents to embrace the project (see Figure 6.5).

What We Notice About Leo Lionni

- Leo's illustrations are remarkable. (They sort of remind us of Eric Carle!) He uses collages to create lots of pretty scenes of animals. He uses watercolors. Some of his pictures seem to "morph" into each other, and the animals' and scenes' colors run into each other.
- Many of his stories are about friends helping friends—all the characters so far have been animals.
- His stories make us happy; but there are parts that "worry" us, like the box of animals to be thrown away and the fish that jumps out of the water before he is rescued.
- He sometimes uses repeating words and alliteration.
- He throws in a little bit of magic—like the lizard.

Home/School Connections
for the Week of October 14–20

- Enjoy reading—both books of choice and books by your expert project author. Be sure to list those books on your October reading log.
- Spend some time talking with your parents about your author and what you notice from book to book. I hope you will notice some similarities. Be thinking of what strategies you can mimic in your own original book! (This part should be fun! We do these often in writing workshop.)

Speaking of academic growth, we are approaching one of my favorite studies ever— our author expert projects! Please see the accompanying criteria that the children helped create for the project. We're going to the library next Friday, and that will be

---

Figure 6.5

continues

the perfect time to gather more of the author's works. Please note that your child does not have to read every single word of these works by themselves. However, they should be very familiar with these books and the author's style of writing. Remember when we all learned about Jan Brett?

1. The children noticed how her illustrations gave clues to what was happening in the story.
2. She also visited the habitats of her stories so she could write and draw realistically.

The expert project has evolved over the years, as we have seen the huge impact that studying authors closely has had on the children's own writing. For the project, they are to identify at least three things they notice about that author's style and then mimic the style in a book they write themselves! As you continue reading about your child's author, as well as the author's stories, talk with your child about things they notice the author doing. Remind them to think deeply. In the next couple of weekly newsletters we will identify various authors and our observations of them, just to give you some ideas.

To date, these are the authors the children are researching and mimicking (so far, everyone has gotten their first choice!):

Laura Numeroff (Hannah)	Dr. Seuss (Garrett)
Cynthia Rylant (Natalie)	Ann M. Martin (Jackson)
Jane O'Connor (Serenity)	Gertrude Chandler Warner (Simon)
Mary Pope Osborne (Brandon H.)	Margaret Rey (Devin)
Eric Carle (Sierra)	Bill Martin, Jr. (Ethan)
Beverly Cleary (Trevor)	Erica Silverman (Bay)
E. B. White (Jayden)	Seymour Simon (Brandon G.)
P. D. Eastman (James)	Barbara Park (Sam)
Jan Brett (Allie)	Meg Cabot (Alana)
Eric Hill (Evelyn)	Frank Asch (Reagan)

Aren't these wonderful authors? Please note that this project can't be put together quickly at the last minute. Begin reading those books now (many of you already have). Enjoy just talking about the things that are cool and unique, things that their favorite authors do.

Figure 6.5 continued

Children teach their classmates about an author and inspire them to read books by this author for themselves. Many kids in the class begin choosing authors featured in expert projects for their independent reading. Author expert projects are also videotaped, and parents are asked to view the video with their children and respond with three pluses and a wish/goal. We want everyone—teachers, parents, children—to reflect on strengths first, then envision a wish or goal. The point is to build on the good, and Sam Goldberg's mother did just that (see Figure 6.6).

Reflect Critically to Deepen and Broaden the Curriculum

Although the new Common Core standards promote critical reflection and opinion writing, the Center for Inquiry headed in this direction long ago. We want children to question what they read, what they think they know, what others tell them, and what our culture conveys. We want them to reach their own informed opinions. We want them to think critically and strategically.

"Our Three Plusses and a Wish"
Evaluation for Expert Projects

Name of Presenting Child: Sam Goldberg
Name of Assessor: Lisa Goldberg
Relationship of Assessor to Child Presenter: Mom
Date: 11/7
Project Title: Barbara Park

- I loved your Book! It was funny, and it really sounded like something Barbara Park would write. The illustrations were funny too.

- You talked about extra things that were n't on your Board, like how she is 3yrs younger than your Nana.

- I like how you told the story about how she used to hide in the hamper and that is why she put Junie B. in the hamper in "Sneaky Peeky Spy" Book.

Wish:

- face the camera more and don't feel like you have to point to each word.

Figure 6.6

Critical reflection may come naturally for some children, but many need repeated, firsthand experiences with the process. They need low-risk scaffolds. They need to construct and shape opinions, and then try them out in the company of others who won't judge them but will ask genuine questions that give them authentic practice explaining their thinking.

Scott Johnson does this in a social studies unit on discovery and the Age of Exploration. As we know too well, we have created underserving cultural icons by misreading history or favoring some perspectives while dismissing others. To help children reflect on historical information critically, Scott composes two very different opinion pieces about Christopher Columbus (see Figure 6.7). He reads both pieces and asks his fourth graders to select one that resonates with them. In small groups, they first discuss why their piece has value given everything they have learned about that time and place in history. Then he has each group present and defend their opinions to the other groups. Through this, Scott teaches his students to think critically about one man in history while giving them practice in adopting and defending opinions.

INTRODUCTION 1

The Age of Exploration is considered a great period of exploration, colonization, and technological advances. One of the true founding fathers of this period is Christopher Columbus. A great admiral, a great sailor, he dominated the seas between 1492 and 1504. It was his courage and determination that inspired an entire age— the Age of Exploration. Christopher Columbus rightly deserves the praise he has received for his great accomplishments.

INTRODUCTION 2

It has been argued that Christopher Columbus was the inspiration for a great period of exploration and colonization. It was he who helped to push technological advances in navigation. It was he who nudged others to join him on his quest to conquer the seas. But it was Columbus who inspired a generation of explorers to conquer, dominate, and destroy. It was Columbus who inspired a generation of explorers, lured by their lust for gold and other treasures, to turn into slave traders. Christopher Columbus does not deserve any title that exemplifies him as a leader, admiral of the seas, or even hero. Christopher Columbus should be remembered as a tyrant whose greed destroyed generations of Native Americans and wiped out entire civilizations.

Figure 6.7 Perspectives on Columbus

Reflect Critically to Challenge the Status Quo

Chris Hass regularly constructs opportunities for his students to confront preconceived notions of what is "normal" so they will learn to understand and value others rather than judge or dismiss them. As part of a unit of study centered on normalcy, Chris and his second graders studied various cultures. Knowing the value of primary sources, Chris invited a number of guests to speak to the class about their own experiences being from, visiting, or being intimately connected with various cultures around the world.

His colleague Tameka Breland eloquently began by saying, "I can't tell you what African American culture means to everyone, but I can talk about what it means to me." (See Figure 6.8.)

As the guests shared and responded to children's insights and questions, Chris charted their collective thinking. The chart (see Figure 6.9) became a touchstone, reminding children of the hazards of stereotypes and the thrill of outgrowing their acceptance of them. The children learned much about the complexity and beauty of diverse people and

Figure 6.8

places while seeing the value of adopting a critical stance toward generalizations. (Chris's complete unit of study is discussed in Chapter 8.)

Reflect on Growth and Change in Student-Led Conferences

For a week or two before student-led conferences in the early spring, students in all the Center's classrooms, K–5, spend a couple of hours each day examining artifacts that best reflect their growth as readers, writers, mathematicians, scientists, social scientists, and community members. This act of looking back to move forward is profound. As students study themselves, they outgrow themselves by identifying their strengths as well as their struggles and envisioning new possibilities. They see how they can learn from their mistakes or miscues. They get in touch with the learning process and themselves as learners. They set new goals for themselves.

Some teachers might balk at taking so much time to prepare for this annual celebratory ritual, but once they live through the process they realize how much revisiting key curricular experiences solidifies and deepens children's learning.

Teachers create templates with guiding questions, often with input from their students, to help them remember and document what they have learned during the year. Like re-reading a book or seeing a movie twice, children notice new things through their second encounter. It's generative to consider and then reconsider the knowledge they've constructed individually and collectively. Students see themselves in new ways.

The children's reflective conversations, documented learning, and self-selected artifacts reveal critical information for teachers as kid watchers. Teachers get another genuine glimpse into what matters most to their students. They learn more about the impact of their teaching moves and curricular decisions.

Culture	Learned	Stereotypes	What We Think
Somali-Bantu	There was a war in Somalia and some people had to leave to stay safe. They lived in a refugee camp for 12 years, in part because America was afraid to bring Muslims here after 9/11. When they came, everyone who helped them learned how beautiful, strong, smart, and caring the Somali families were.	Because they were Muslims some people were afraid of them. Some people thought all Muslims were terrorists or hated America. THIS IS UNTRUE.	"I used to think Muslims were bad but that was before I knew. Now I know they're loving and have a big heart." —Rachael
Ecuador	Ecuador is a country with many resources like oil/agriculture (crops). There are well-known writers and artists. They do not eat out as often as we do—only for special occasions. There are rich people, poor people, and people in between—just like here.	Some people think all Latin Americans are from Mexico. There are many Spanish-speaking countries in Central and South America.	Ecuador has a lot to offer the world that we didn't even know about.
France	Many of our words came from French. France is a very old country with buildings that are sometimes as much as 2,000 years old. French culture can be different from one region of the country to another.	None	France has a lot of history and an interesting culture.

Figure 6.9 Moving Beyond Stereotypes   *continues*

Culture	Learned	Stereotypes	What We Think
South Africa	Apartheid separated blacks, whites, Indians, and "colored." Apartheid kept people poor while others stayed rich. Townships and shantytowns. People are nice and share what they have.	All countries in Africa are the same.	The government should help the poor improve their lives with safe houses and jobs.
China	Use symbols to write. Put their last name first. Southern China eats lots of rice and Northern China eats lots of noodles. Sit in rows of desks at school. Many had a picture of an old president. The Forbidden City is revered by many in China.	All Chinese are smart. They are well mannered. People in China are all poor.	"I thought they were poor at first but then I read some books and found out not everyone is." —Ryan
Libya	Big cities that looked clean. Read right to left. Write in Arabic. 17th largest country in the world based on size of land.	It is all desert and people live in tent-like homes. Libyans kidnap people.	We're surprised to find that they eat similar foods.

Figure 6.9 Moving Beyond Stereotypes, continued

Teachers launch the process by asking their kids to look through collections of their work—to remember where they've been in order to consider where they're going. Then, together, they generate class lists of content explored, questions pursued, and strategies employed. They often chart the ideas generated during these whole-class conversations.

Then the children personalize it, deciding what they want to say and do to show their parents how they have grown and changed as readers, writers, mathematicians, scientists, and social scientists. Sometimes this means reading excerpts from books they read at the beginning of the year and then sharing examples of texts they are currently reading. At other times it means conducting an experiment and explaining how the process works. Still other times it means showing how to solve a math problem in several ways.

Teachers often bind the children's reflections in a booklet the children can use as a guide during the conference. Although they are encouraged to "speak from their hearts," the booklets help students remember what they want to say and stay focused and organized during their twenty-minute presentations. These booklets often become treasured keepsakes for families. It's easy and incredibly satisfying to map the children's growth over time through these documents and corresponding artifacts.

Jennifer Barnes finds a prompt in the National Council of Teachers of English Reading Initiative materials very helpful in inspiring children to reflect on their growth: "If you want to know about me as a _____, you need to know . . ." Her kindergartners and first graders complete one of these templates the day before they launch their conferences (see the examples in Figure 6.10).

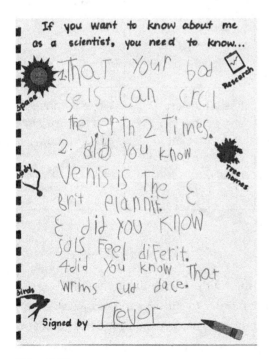
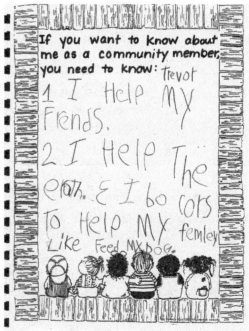

Figure 6.10

Each year Susanne Pender constructs a reflective group template for and with her students, something that truly reflects the class's unique interests, strengths, and personality. She shows the students examples from previous classes to help them envision the possibilities. After some focused exploration, she and her students create the template. Completed examples are shown in Figure 6.11.

Thinking Like a Reader Kenton

3 words that describe me as a reader are...
Unstoppable
Risk Taker
text to text

3 ways I have grown as a reader are...
Going to harder books.
like I used to read books with only
5 pages now I read chapter books
I know more words. Now I'm reading My Weird
School like I didn't now how to spell
forgotten now I do. I look at
smaller detail to make it come
together. I go to website and
read to know about the
world like my P.I.P.

Artifacts I will use include...
Sign of the Beaven
My Weider school

An important book for me this year OR my favorite types of books I read are...
Because...
My Wierder School series
beCause it's funny and has
mysteries. Sign of the Beaven
becau they help eachother Matt
helps Attean and Attean helps
Matt.

My goal for myself as a reader is...
Try my best not to get a
word wrong and more nonfition
books like Green land to keep
going deeper.

Thinking Like a Reader Madison

3 words that describe me as a reader are...
linguistC A Person who Studies words and language
risk taker mentor.

3 ways I have grown as a reader are...
one way I have grown as a reader is I used
to only read fairy books but now I am reading nancy
Drew books. Another way I have grown
as a reader is, if I don't get what I read
I go back and re-read it. I also have learned
to stop at the end of a page and look
over it to make sure I got all of it.

Artifacts I will use include...
Nancy Drew books and fairy books.

Figure 6.11

The fourth- and fifth-grade teachers engage their students in similar reflections, with the expectation that their work will be more sophisticated than when they were younger and their presentations will include new ways to show what they know. Tameka Breland's students focus on what they enjoyed learning and why, as well as the artifact or demonstration they will use to show or demonstrate their growth (see Figure 6.12).

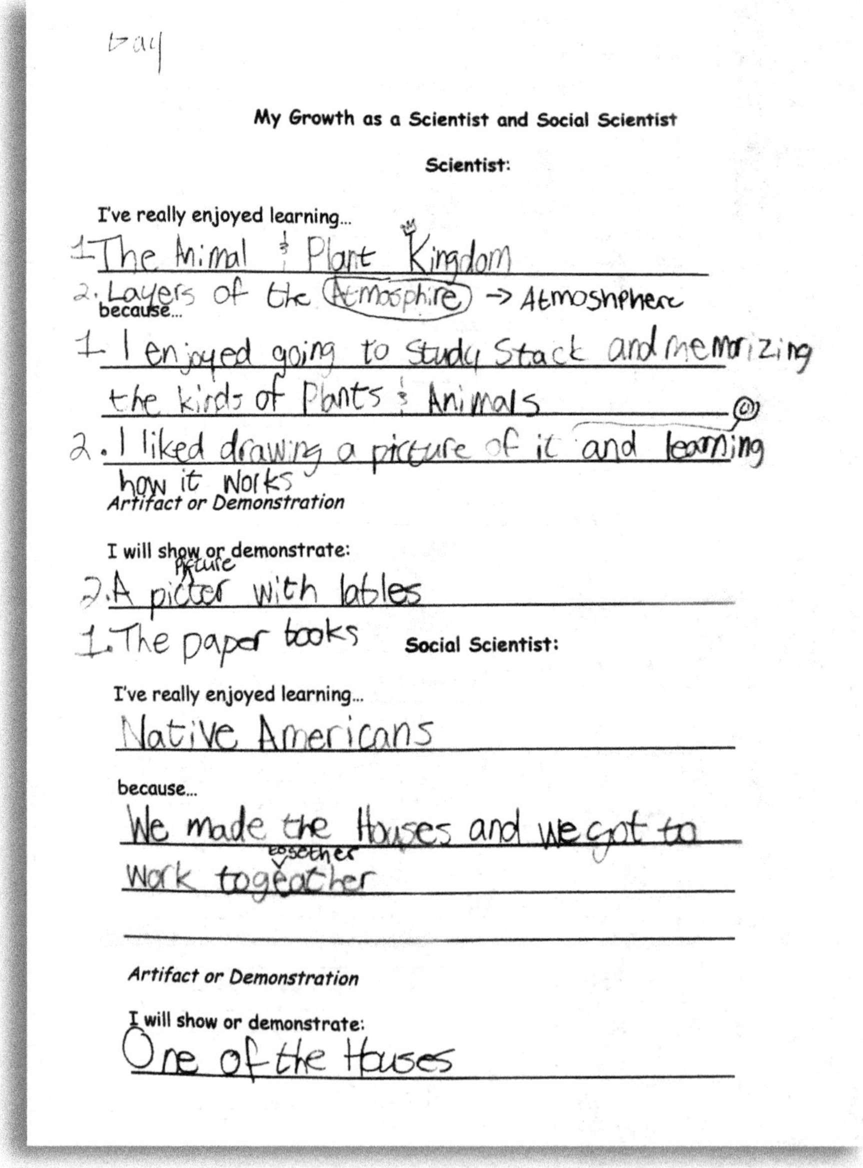

bay

My Growth as a Scientist and Social Scientist

Scientist:

I've really enjoyed learning...

1. The Animal & Plant Kingdom
2. Layers of the (Atmoophire) → Atmoshpherc

because...

1. I enjoyed going to study Stack and memorizing the kinds of Plants & Animals
2. I liked drawing a picture of it and learning how it Works

Artifact or Demonstration

I will show or demonstrate:

2. A picter (picture) with lables
1. The paper books

Social Scientist:

I've really enjoyed learning...

Native Americans

because...

We made the Houses and we got to Work togeather (together)

Artifact or Demonstration

I will show or demonstrate:

One of the Houses

Figure 6.12

Figure 6.13

Figure 6.14

One thing I love most about working with my colleagues at the Center for Inquiry is how teachers take insights and ideas and make them their own in their own way. They are always devising new practices based on the beliefs that ground our school culture. Amanda Mahowald and her fifth graders surprised parents this year by showing their growth during the year on websites. Individual pages represented who they were as readers, writers, mathematicians, scientists, and social scientists. They learned about technology while using it as a tool to capture and display their learning within and across content areas. Anagraciela's home page began, "Dear Mommy and Antonio, Hello and surprise! You thought that I was going to give you a booklet, right? Well this is the surprise J. Welcome to my website!" (See Figure 6.13.)

CFI teachers do everything they can to make student-led conferences both informative and memorable. Some teachers videotape the conferences, others send home artifacts and booklets that showcase children's growth, and still others take photographs during the conferences as memory placeholders. Michelle Kimpson took photos of her kindergartners and their families this year (see Figure 6.14).

Many teachers also invite parents to bring a letter celebrating their child's growth and change to the conference. Some parents read the letters aloud; others gently place them in their children's hands. The content and form of the letters are as diverse as the families. All are treasures, because parents' perspectives on their precious children are revealing and touching. Although each teacher makes student-led conferences their own, these conferences are a gift to everyone at the school, a reminder of what matters most: the children.

Set Goals and Reflect on Successes and Challenges to Build and Sustain Classroom Community

Although this book has focused on the power of inquiry to both inform and transform learners and learning, inquiry to build community is equally effective. Fourth- and fifth-grade teacher Scott Johnson has helped everyone connected with CFI recognize the importance of using reflection to improve individual and community interaction. Scott's students had become masters of saying all the right things, but they were not living the vision they proclaimed. So he designed a project to help his students take deliberate action as a result of their talk.

They begin each day by setting individual and class goals and then documenting them on sticky notes. They carry their sticky notes with them throughout the day ("Post-its® in their pockets") as constant, concrete reminders of what they need to work on individually and collectively. At the end of the day, the class forms a closing circle during which they reflect on and honestly share whether they accomplished their goals or not. Let's listen in on one:

Scott: Share whether you reached your goal today or not. If you reached it or did not, just share a few reasons why you thought you did or didn't as well. We'll also talk about our class goal of not speaking over each other.

Haley: My goal was to pay attention on the rug and at our seats, and I think I accomplished it. Sometimes I might be silly with my friends and I don't think I did that much today.

Megan: My goal was to pay attention to the person who is speaking, and I think I accomplished it.

Ronan: My goal was to say please and thank you, and I don't think I accomplished it yet.

Scott: It's not an easy goal is it?

Ryan: My goal was to participate in more conversations, and I did.

Caleb: My goal was not to talk over each other, and I accomplished it.

Kyle: My goal was to pay attention on the rug, and I accomplished it because I usually sit by Caleb and whisper and I didn't today.

David: Mine was not to talk at inappropriate times, and I don't think I accomplished it because I talked over people.

Scott: It's important that you realized that.

Because of the strong sense of community Scott and the other teachers create in their classrooms, students are open and honest about their successes and nonsuccesses. They have learned the value of approximations in learning new content and strategies, and Scott helps them realize that the same process applies to behavior and interaction. All learners, tall and small, need to study themselves if they are to grow. By doing so they became better community members and more engaged, attentive learners.

Share End-of-Year Reflections with Parents

Clearly, reflection is a habit of the heart and mind at the Center for Inquiry. It's woven into the curriculum, ongoing assessments, and parent communications. Tim O'Keefe's end-of-year letter (Figure 6.15) reveals the content and spirit of these reflective tools and the power of reflection itself.

While every day in the life of a student (and a teacher) isn't always pure joy, I think we had a tremendously successful year (and it was mostly fun). We covered a lot of curriculum but, more important, we uncovered a lot of really important learning. We watched as caterpillars hatched and began to grow, and grow, and grow. We watched as they climbed to the top of their enclosure and shed their skin for the final time. We waited patiently for the larvae to emerge as beautiful swallowtail butterflies. It took only a couple of weeks for some to emerge; it took several months for others. The last one came out just a couple of weeks ago. We met and fell in love with Molly Sanders and Madona Sedhom and watched them grow and change and become wonderful teachers. We shared awesome books, outgrew ourselves as writers, scientists, mathematicians. We watched the news and the polls and the election results as South Carolina elected its first woman to the governor's office. We had interesting visitors, took part in some terrific field studies, created surveys and graphs, and shared excellent questions and observations about the world in our class journals. It is these critical incidents in the life of a teacher that make each year unique. This year was filled with special learning, from literature studies to expert projects to science demonstrations. This year was filled with special people as well. From our MAT Tall Teachers to our pen pals to parents who came in to help out with a workshop, our classroom community was enriched by others who devoted time, thought, and care to our learning.

In some ways we were like those caterpillars, not really knowing what to expect from this year. But we grew and changed and matured. We became more efficient mathematicians, more effective readers, more curious about the world, clearer writers, better team members, wiser teachers, better researchers, more fearless at asking questions. In so many ways we shed our old skins and just grew up a little. And after 32 years in the business, I did too.

Figure 6.15

Make Reflection a Habit in Your Classroom

To bring inquiry as a way of being into your classroom, it is essential to weave reflection into your curriculum and culture. When teachers and learners make a habit of reflecting individually and collectively, everyone becomes more aware of how readers, writers, mathematicians, scientists, and social scientists think, work, and communicate. This awareness allows us to construct a vision of where we are as learners and what we need to do to continue growing and changing. In cultures that support genuine inquiry, everyone is expected to grow and change. It's not about comparing students with one another. Rather, it's about honestly creating a vision of what is possible for learning and learners and deliberately working toward the vision through reflective engagements that track and promote change.

One of the best ways to create a classroom culture of inquiry is to build formal reflection into your workshops, assessment strategies, standards analysis, curriculum, and community-building activities. As you begin envisioning your daily and long-range plans, ask yourself questions like these:

- Am I making space in reading, writing, math, and other workshops for students to reflect in the midst of their learning as well as after the fact?
- Do my assessment strategies promote reflection and self-evaluation?
- Might I invite children and parents to reflect on and celebrate growth and change by videotaping expert project presentations or instituting student-led conferences?
- Do I regularly ask myself, or my students, to take a critical stance toward knowledge? Do I help students to form, critique, and share opinions and information verbally and through clear, compelling writing?
- Am I fostering inquiry into our community or classroom interactions in the same ways I promote curriculum inquiry?
- Most important, am I making space in my daily life to reflect, to wonder, to treasure the gift of living, learning, and growing in front of and alongside my students?

Reflection matters only if it leads to new, strategic, informed actions. As the Talmud expresses so eloquently, "To look is one thing, to see is another, to understand what you see is a third. To learn from what you understand is still something else. But to act on what you learn is all that really matters."

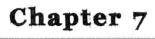

Chapter 7

Planning for Inquiry

The processes of inquiry are implied in all instruction, but too often they're invisible to students. And yet our desire for kids to lead inquiring lives doesn't mean that we can impose the processes of inquiry on them. Teachers need to create opportunities for students to name and experience the processes of inquiry through integrated units of study. When students are given careful scaffolding and space for their input along the way, they share questions, insights, and connections that are beyond (and often better than) what you could have imagined.

Embedded Inquiry, Not Open Inquiry

> *Design is the application of intent—the opposite of happenstance, and an antidote to accident.*
> —ROBERT L. PETERS

In our effort to offer students choice and ownership in the curriculum, we can overcompensate by making our invitations *too* open. When studying nonfiction text features and structures, we may invite children to choose their own topic and then explore how nonfiction texts are organized and how messages or content are most effectively communicated. While admirable, it primarily promotes learning about nonfiction as traditionally addressed in language arts: kids will pick up interesting ideas about their topic, but content is secondary.

The power of choice and ownership can still exist when we embed an inquiry into strategies for reading and writing nonfiction texts within content-rich units of study in the sciences or social sciences. When we do, we can teach content and non-fiction simultaneously. We can make stronger, more explicit connections when kids are thinking together about a topic, concept, or theme. Students can move in and out of mentor and apprentice roles, and everyone can contribute, even the young-est. With support, any student can do this work. But what do we mean by support? In the introduction, I shared how I was changed by studying the moon alongside Susan Bolte and her first graders. Now you'll get to see how her students were changed, too. You will see how Susan planned her astronomy unit and the student work it inspired. You will see the power of teaching processes (how to learn), nonfiction, and content together in a video clip of first graders sharing their moon journals. For a download-able version of the planning template, and for Susan's complete unit and video clip, go to www.heinemann.com/products/E04603.aspx.

From Inspiration to Reflection: Making a Unit Work

Our best planning comes from making predictions and creating conditions for students to engage in particular kinds of thinking (strategies, skills, and content connections). Curriculum is the transaction that occurs among teacher, students, and resources within and across curricular structures. As Carolyn Burke taught us, the best plans are written in pencil. The teacher plans ahead—creating a unit that describes experiences and goals—but then plans daily, adapting and creating minilessons to meet the needs of students. This transaction is possible when teachers are committed to teaching responsively. We don't simply teach reading, writing, mathematics, science, and social studies; we teach readers, writers, mathematicians, scientists, and social scientists by working within an apprenticeship model. We work in front of, alongside, and behind the children as the adult, experienced mentor in the classroom. The apprenticeship model means we devote as much time and care into teaching children *how* to learn as *what* to learn, and we teach processes and content simultaneously.

We devote the majority of our time to teaching integrated units of study within the context of what we have traditionally called science or social studies. However, we also capitalize on other curricular structures, such as reading and writing workshops, to extend content learning through content literacy work. (Chapter 8 gives an in-depth explanation of curricular structures and the diverse roles they play in a comprehensive curriculum.) In this chapter you will see how Susan Bolte accesses reading, writing, and science workshops as well as morning meetings to teach content and content literacy across the day (see Figure 7.1).

What Do We Believe?

We begin planning by reflecting on what we believe about our students and how to best support their growth and change within the context of particular units of study. When we name our beliefs, we are deliberate about living into them with our students, day in and day out. Do our beliefs and practices match? This process pushes our growth as teachers. While many beliefs about how children learn are universal, different units of study offer different opportunities to address beliefs that are unique to the sciences or social sciences.

Here are Susan's beliefs about teaching her students as young astronomers:

1. Children are by nature curious. They are aware of the presence of the sun, moon, and stars, and have many questions about these objects they see in the sky.
2. Children care about the world they live in. As they discover more about the special place we call home (Earth), they will be even more enthusiastic and intentional about caring for our planet.
3. It is important that children learn to use authentic tools (binoculars, telescopes, scientific journals, and measuring tools) as they work as scientists.
4. It is necessary to give children time to spend exploring and thinking about the things they are learning.
5. Children learn best when they contribute to the learning by bringing in resources and information from home.
6. Children learn best when they are fully immersed in the unit of study (literature, nonfiction texts, sign-in graphs, student-made art and other room displays, resources from home, music, physical activities, etc.).
7. Children love to play and have fun, and they learn best when they are enjoying and interacting with the subject matter.
8. Children learn best when they have an "emotional hook" to hang knowledge on.

8:00–8:45   Crossing the Threshold, Beginning Our Day Together
- Welcome, folders, sign in, bathroom, water
- Read aloud
- School announcements
- Morning meeting
- Morning message
- Greeting
- Share and news

8:45–9:30   Writing Workshop
- Demonstration: Minilesson
- Engagement (living the process)
- Reflection (reflecting as individuals and/or groups on the content skills, strategies, and concepts)
- Celebration (giving public recognition for growth and change)

9:30–10:20   Special Areas

10:20–11:05   Unit of Study in Science or Social Studies

11:05–11:50   Explorations

11:50–12:20   Lunch

12:30–1:30   Reading Workshop
- Read aloud or shared reading
- Independent reading
- Buddy reading
- Book recommendation
- Strategy share
- Book selection

1:30–2:10   Recess

2:10–2:40   Math Workshop
- What do you notice about this number?
- Hands-on activity
- Word problem
- Pictorial and abstract representation

2:40–2:50   Closing Circle
- What I learned
- What was interesting
- What went well
- What I will do the same or different tomorrow

2:50   Dismissal

Figure 7.1 Susan's Daily Forecast in First Grade

Planning at the belief level rather than at the activity level ensured that Susan's teaching supported the learning she hoped her students would do. Now let's see how Susan brought these beliefs to life during the unit.

Which Standards Will Be "Uncovered"?

First, envision authentic, meaningful possibilities for teaching and learning, and *then* consult the standards to decide how they might be met in authentic ways. Our best teaching moves grow out of *uncovering,* not simply covering, the standards. If you find a void between your vision and the standards, you simply regroup and plan engagements that will fill the void. You strike that balance between what you are required to teach and what you need to do to bring joyful, rigorous learning to life. That's authentic accountability. Some teachers prefer to cut and paste the official standards directly into the template, while others translate the standards into their own words for efficiency and clarity. Units are interdisciplinary, so we look across content areas for standards (see Figure 7.2).

Grade 1, South Carolina Standards

Earth Science: Sun and Moon

Standard 1-3: The student will demonstrate an understanding of the features of the sky and the patterns of the sun and the moon.

Indicators

1–3.1 Compare the features of the day and night sky.

1–3.2 Recall that the sun is a source of heat and light for Earth.

1–3.3 Recognize that the sun and the moon appear to rise and set.

1–3.4 Illustrate changes in the moon's appearance (including patterns over time).

ELA: Understanding and Using Informational Texts

Standard 1-1: The student will read and comprehend a variety of informational texts in print and nonprint formats.

Standard 1-5: The student will write for a variety of purposes and audiences.

Standard 1-6: The student will access and use information from a variety of sources.

Figure 7.2

What Questions Do We Want to Investigate?

After identifying which standards you'll embed in a unit, you'll want to think about what's behind the standards and what other kinds of thinking, conversations, and learning strategies you want to promote. To help get there, we use a set of general guiding questions to help generate questions specific to the unit topic (see Figure 7.3). The questions we ask influence what we see. Guiding questions help teachers and students see the world in new ways. The list of questions provided is not a mandate; rather, it is intended to stimulate a range of possibilities. For instance, we have found conceptual questions around diversity, democracy, systems, balance, cycles, change, and voice to be incredibly powerful. Pragmatic questions help students get below the surface to consider how the knowledge under study was generated and the tentative nature of knowledge in general. Of course, it is critical to urge students to pose personal questions like "Why does it matter to me?" and social questions like "Why does it matter in the world?" Finally, we want students to develop a habit of posing questions that promote social action, questions such as "So what?" "Now what?" and "How might we make the world a better place by taking action on what we have learned?"

Here are the questions Susan thought were important for her students to explore as astronomers:

1. What have we already noticed about the day and night sky?
2. What do we already know about the universe and our own solar system?
3. Why do we want to learn about our solar system and the universe?
4. What questions do we have?
5. How can we use the information we gain to make our world a better place?
6. How has our understanding of astronomy changed over time?
7. How do we learn about things that we previously had little or no knowledge of?
8. What is the difference between a primary and a secondary source?
9. What is the solar system?
10. How does the sun produce heat and light?
11. Why are heat and light important to us on Earth?
12. What is photosynthesis and how does it relate to the sun?
13. What is the difference between a solar and a lunar eclipse?
14. What effect does the moon have on Earth?
15. What are the "phases of the moon?"

Conceptual

- Perspectives: Which perspectives (reader, writer, mathematician, scientist, and/or social scientist) offer potential insights or strategies for investigating this unit of study? That is, what questions would a social scientist ask and how might she investigate this issue? What questions would a mathematician ask?
- Systems: What systems are involved in this unit and how are they related?
- Cycles: Are there cycles embedded in this unit of study? How might we gain a deeper understanding of the unit by investigating the natural and man-made cycles?
- Change: Has change occurred over time in relation to this unit of study? If so, how might studying the natural or man-made changes help us better understand the topic?
- Voice: Whose voice is heard or privileged? Whose voice is absent or silenced?
- Power: How might power structures help us better understand this issue?

Pragmatic/Universal

- Who developed the idea, invention, or concept?
- Why was the idea or invention created? What was the purpose of the invention given the context and culture of the time period?
- Where did the knowledge or information presented in the materials we are reading in this unit of study come from? Can we trust or believe it? Do we need to access multiple sources to triangulate our knowledge or understanding?
- Have common knowledge, beliefs, or understandings about this topic changed over time? What led to shifts in our beliefs or understandings?

Personal Knowledge

- Why does this knowledge or information matter to me?
- How has what I have learned during this unit changed me?

Social Knowledge

- Why does the knowledge I'm learning in this unit of study matter in the world?

From Personal Knowledge to Social Action

- So what?
- Now what? How might we take action on what we have learned during this unit of study?
- How might we show or demonstrate what we have learned during this unit to others?

Figure 7.3 Possible Guiding Questions for Planning

16. What do we know about travel to the moon?

17. What does the term atmosphere refer to?

18. What is the Earth made of?

19. Why do we experience day and night and the changing of
    the seasons?

20. What other planets exist in our solar system?

21. What is the difference between the solar system, the Milky Way
    galaxy, other galaxies, and the universe? How does this knowledge
    help us understand life on our planet?

22. What are asteroids, comets, and meteors?

23. How can studying space help us understand the past?

24. How can what we've learned help us plan for the future?

Susan knew that some questions would become more important to her students than others and that they would generate questions of their own. Of course, they did! These new questions are one of the ways we measure students' growth and change through the course of the unit. Next you will see the kinds of questions that children posed as astronomers in their class journal and on sticky notes as they read and talked about nonfiction texts. Susan's questions helped her design learning engagements that would uncover standards in authentic ways, offering guidance and unity as she moved from her unit plan to daily plans. Susan collaborated with her students by inviting them to generate questions, too. She did so by making space in the daily life of her classroom for kids to pose and explore questions they pondered. She used a large class journal to capture children's questions and answers over time.

Using Reading and Writing to Pose and Ponder Kids' Questions During Science Workshop: Class Journals

Susan had her students pose questions in a class space journal every day. In the beginning she was the scribe; later, students entered the questions themselves. They left blank space between the questions so they could return and answer them as they read about and investigated the universe (see Figure 7.4).

Susan gave them thirty minutes a day to "muck around" with nonfiction books during science workshop to research their questions individually and collectively. They documented what they learned on sticky notes. In Susan's words, "We made a habit of keeping our research together in our class book about the solar system. Our book became a resource for us" (see Figure 7.5).

Questions we have about space:

① How was the moon created?
Kierra There are different theories but most astronomers think an asteroid hit the earth causing some of the earth to break off. This part became the sun.

② How many people have stepped on the moon?
Tucker

③ Why can astronauts jump so high on the moon?
Lyn Astronauts can jump higher on the moon than on earth because the moon is smaller an has less gravity to hold the astronauts down

④ How did Pluto become not a planet
Joshua size and orbit (see above)

⑤ How does the moon and sun take t)e going around?
Kinna The moon orbits the earth and the earth orbits the sun.

⑥ What was the first planet discovered
Mikaela

⑦ How was the Earth created?
Modison

⑧ What causes the seasons?
Susan The earth is tilted on its axis so that a the earth it revolves around the sun, different parts it closer to the sun, causing the seasons

⑨ Does the Earth and Moon and Sun all spin around each other? Johnathan No,
08/22

Figure 7.4

We did ReSrch at School

Ayshng-31-11
I notin
a Bota Metter
is the First
Plonat ni
the color
X eistem the

Weny a Edith
Mars & Jupite
Saturn uronus
neptune sun
Moon
Auztin
8-31-11

mars is dry and
dusty
Keaton 8-31-11

Do you Christon
See the
Moon in
the night sky

Keaton 8-31-11
mars looks
red from space

Figure 7.5

Susan taught her students to take notes by taking notes herself. She demonstrated how she used notes to remember important facts and invited the children to try out her process as they read. Students squealed with delight when they uncovered an answer to a question that one of their friends had posted in the class journal.

Susan also built reflection into the daily routine, asking students to share "fast facts" as well as strategies they used to capture big ideas on sticky notes. The small notes helped the kids recognize the need to synthesize information and put ideas into their own words.

The class developed such a passion for their new learning that they began doing their own research at home. Susan created a section in the class space journal for kids to paste in their new learning and gave them daily opportunities to share their self-directed homework orally as well. In inquiry-based classrooms, it's cool to know things, and class journals like Susan's encourage kids to document and share their new insights.

How Will They Investigate These Questions During Science Workshop?

It's not enough to simply ask questions. As you plan, you want to think of experiences and methods—observations, interviews, experiments, surveys, and controlled studies—that will offer students firsthand opportunities to explore these questions. Students learn best when we teach the skillfulness of inquiry authentically, across contexts and over time. Therefore, it helps to sketch out possible methods of investigation that will promote content learning and teach the skillfulness of inquiry at the same time. We want our students to learn how to make careful observations, conduct interviews, design surveys, and perform experiments and controlled studies. Although it's essential that we teach kids how to use reading and writing as tools for learning, it is equally important that they do more than learn vicariously. We want them to have firsthand opportunities to investigate, collect, and interpret qualitative and quantitative data; to learn when to access primary and secondary sources; and to think and analyze complex issues for themselves.

Here are some of the invitations Susan created to investigate questions that young astronomers ask:

- We create moon craters.
  - *Fill paper bowls with plaster of paris.*
  - *Drop marbles and rocks into the plaster from varying heights, while making predictions about the type of craters that might be formed.*
  - *Spray the plaster with water until soaked and allow to dry.*
  - *Paint to realistically represent the moon surface.*
- We invite a guest to speak with us about the moon and its effect on the Earth. We hope to learn about the elliptical orbit of the moon, the perigee, the apogee, and the effect of the full moon on the tides and currents.
- As we focus on the mythology behind some of the constellations, the students create "view finders" that represent different constellations. The children punch holes in black paper that covers a paper towel roll. We paint one day and create the constellations on the following day.
- We talk about the theories of how the planets were formed. We try to "make a planet" by rolling clay across a surface covered with flour. We use this as a visual to help us understand how planets grow bigger as the gravity that surrounds them pulls dust and gas toward them.

- We examine the Earth's atmosphere (the layer of air that surrounds our planet) by lighting several candles, putting jars of different sizes over them, and watching to see how long they burn.
  - *"Let's work together to figure out how we can demonstrate that the Earth's atmosphere contains oxygen. Here are our supplies: different size jars, candles, a tray, and matches. What do we already know about oxygen? What did we notice? Why did some burn out faster? Let's spend a little time talking about oxygen and carbon dioxide . . . . I wonder: Do other planets have atmospheres? Are they made up of the same gases that make up Earth's atmosphere?"*

- We explore how clouds are formed by filling a glass with ice water and letting it sit for 30 minutes. We look at the outside of the glass to see what is happening and talk about how that might relate to cloud formation.

- We examine the layers of a hard-boiled egg and compare them to the layers of the Earth.
  - *Rust: thirty giant slabs or plates of rock that float on the soft, liquid rock below (egg shell)*
  - *Mantle: magma (volcanoes) lava (egg white)*
  - *Outer core: melted metals—soft and liquid iron and nickel (egg yolk)*
  - *Inner core: hard iron and nickel (egg yolk)*

- We inquire into earthquakes and what causes them. We build a town using base-ten blocks, building blocks, toy cars, a wooden train set, and any other items the students choose. Together we simulate one plate of the earth sliding over another plate, causing the ground to shake. We watch to see what happens to our town (the people, the houses, the roads, the power supply, etc.).

- What do the people of the town need after the earthquake? Find Haiti on the map. I show a photograph of our Compassion Child. I share what happened in Haiti almost two years ago. The country was basically destroyed by a very large earthquake.
  - National Geographic *photos and kids' blog http://kidsblogs.national geographic.com/kidsnews/2010/01/haiti-devastated-by-earthquake.html*
  - *Video of the beauty of Haiti and then the destruction of the earthquake www.youtube.com/watch?v=sYNpV_8s4X8&feature=player_embedded*
  - *YouTube video about Andrise*

- www.youtube.com/watch?v=ve0YXqB_93Y
  - *Andrise: one year later www.youtube.com/watch?v=9MiYjcXiNgc&feature=related*
  - *Together we can change the world . . .*
- www.youtube.com/watch?v=qFy54NmYPyc
  - *Do we want to help? What can we do to help?*
- As we learn about the planet Mars, we learn that it is called the "Red Planet." We perform a hands-on experiment as we make predictions about what the reddish substance on a metal disc may be. The children then take turns using a metal brush to remove some of the substance. Eventually, I hope that one of the children guesses that the reddish substance is rust. We then talk about the fact that iron must come in contact with water and oxygen in order to rust. Since rust is found on Mars, we can hypothesize that, at one time, both water and oxygen were on Mars.
- The students present their group projects on the solar system (the sun and everything that orbits it). Parents will be invited to be with us as we learn from each other. We hang our "solar system" from the ceiling and celebrate by sharing foods that the astronauts eat and drink.

Teaching Content and Content Literacy in Concert: It Goes Both Ways

Susan wove content literacy into the fabric of science workshop. She also did the reverse. by using the curricular structures of shared reading and writing workshop to extend their learning about astronomy while teaching her young authors nonfiction text features and text structures. Susan didn't force it. She made seamless curricular moves so children would naturally learn content and content literacy together across curricular structures. At times Susan would draw their attention to the text as young astronomers, and other times as readers and writers. In so doing, she was teaching them how we transact with nonfiction like we do outside of school. As adults, we shift perspectives as readers, writers, and content learners quite fluidly. Susan did just that by teaching content and content literacy across curricular structures.

Shared Reading

Susan used shared reading to teach her young readers to navigate and interpret captions, charts, photographs, models, and narrative text; take notes on interesting new facts; and seek answers to their burning questions. She taught them how to read nonfiction while reading to learn about the universe. Each shared reading experience was unique, but here's a typical one:

Susan (*propping a big book on the easel*): I was listening to you guys as you were reading and it made me think of this other book and it's called—can you tell me what it's called?

Students (*in concert*): *Finding the Moon!*

Susan: And this has a lot of the same information that *Earth and Moon* does, but it takes it to another level; it adds some more information. Where do we usually find the table of contents?

Students: The first page.

Susan: The first page. And we can find it in fiction or nonfiction, right? What do you think this is going to be?

Several kids: Nonfiction.

Susan: Yes. So here it is, "Contents," and then it says, "What do we see in the sky?" So if we wanted to read about that, what page would we turn to?

Students: Two.

Susan: Two. What if we skipped down here to "People in Science" and wanted to read about Neil Armstrong?

Students: Page fourteen.

Susan: Fourteen, okay. [*Notices Lyn is not engaged.*] Lyn, do you remember what a glossary tells us? Let's give Lyn a chance to think. [*Lyn tunes in but does not respond to Susan's question so Susan gives Joshua a nod.*]

Joshua (*after a moment*): There's another word.

Susan: What is the other word?

Joshua: Index.

Susan: There is an index, but what were we talking about? Remember, if you want to look up a general thing, if you want general information, you can look in the table of contents and it will tell you what chapter that's in. If you want specific information, if you just want to know about the North Star, you might look it up in the index. And it will tell you exactly what page. But a glossary, what was the other name for a glossary?

Tucker: Dictionary.

Susan: Dictionary. So if you don't know the meaning of a word, you can turn to the glossary on page sixteen. So if we did that—here we go, "Glossary." [*Turns to a page in the glossary.*] Carter, you're up front, can you read this? What is the definition of the moon?

Carter (*reading*): "The moon is a giant rock that travels around the earth."

Susan: Awesome. Okay. Mikaela, can you read what a sea is? And it might be different than you've ever known it before. What are the seas?

Mikaela: Dark.

Susan: Dark, okay. Evan?

Evan (*reading*): "Flat planets . . ."

Susan: Not planets, plā—

Evan (*reading*): ". . . places on the moon where there is no water."

Susan: Have we ever heard of a sea with no water?

Evan: No.

Susan: Later on we're going to figure out—we'll look up why they call those places seas.

Evan: Let's go to that page.

Susan (*thinking aloud as she explores the text*): Now, seas—uh oh, this book doesn't have an index. Now see, wouldn't it be great to have an index? Because then we would know just what page to go to. But if we know it's a flat place, and this is a book about the moon, we probably can look through the contents. Let's see, "What is the moon like?" Do you think that would be a good place to start?

Students: Yes, page eleven.

Courtney: Ms. Bolte, I have a good idea. Maybe during writing workshop we can make an index book!

Susan: I think that would be an awesome idea. I would like to help some of you index your books.

Goody: What's index mean?

Susan: In the back of most books there is an index. If you want to know about one thing, just one specific little thing, the index tells you exactly what page you can find it on. So page eleven. [*Turns to page eleven and reads.*] "What is the moon like? The moon has no air. The moon has mountains." That's not talking about seas. Here it is, "Seas." [*Underscores the text with a pointer as she reads.*] "The moon has dark, flat places. We call these places seas. But the seas on the moon do not have water." But you know what? I've been doing some research at home, and I found out why they call these dark, flat places seas. But I'll tell you later. But think about it, because you might be able to figure it out on your own.

Carter: I want to call them spots.

Susan: You want to call them spots? It's as good as any name. Okay, so let's read a couple pages of this. We may not get through this whole book today, because I want to show you something special I've been working on.

Susan also taught the children about the tentative nature of knowledge. A few students found conflicting information about Pluto's status as a planet. (Beware of outdated content information in your curriculum materials!) Susan transformed this drama into exciting new learning opportunities via shared reading. The children learned how new tools were invented that allowed astronomers to better understand Pluto. The more scientists learned, the more they realized that it no longer met the criteria of a planet. The kids updated their understanding of planets and learned the value of reading publication dates.

Writing Workshop

During the moon unit, Susan alternated her writing workshops between lessons devoted to teaching craft, genre, revision, or editing and free-choice writing sessions. Invited to select their own topics and genres, the majority of these young authors chose to write about space. That's what happens when children are truly invested in content learning—they see and act on the world with a new lens.

The more the children learned about the sights and sounds of astronomy, the more their personal writing centered on the content and elements of the scientific literature they were devouring individually and collectively. They used models to convey planetary rotations (see Figure 7.6).

Like many young writers, they used lists to convey why they liked the Earth, the sun, the moon, or another planet (see Figure 7.7).

Figure 7.6
Uranus spins sideways
like a somersault like this.

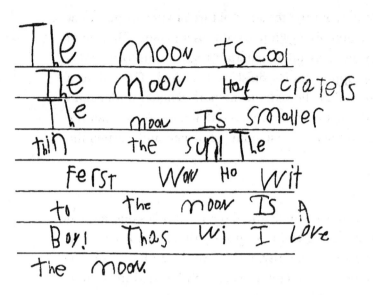

Figure 7.7a
The moon is cool.
The moon has craters.
The moon is smaller than the sun!
The first one who went to the moon is a boy.
That's why I love the moon.

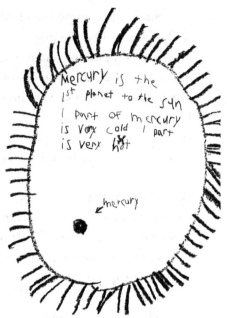

Figure 7.7b
Mercury is the 1st planet to the sun.
1 part of Mercury is very cold. 1 part
is very hot.

These young authors revealed their developing grasp of astronomy. They also conveyed their capacity to capture and share their content learning in ways their non-fiction mentors taught them. Although Susan devoted science workshop to teaching young astronomers, their learning took hold in such profound ways; they used writing workshop to show what they had learned about content and how to write compelling nonfiction texts.

The Momentum of Inquiry

These young astronomers learned a great deal *about* literacy while learning *through* literacy. And although content was central to the success of this unit, their literacy experiences were enhanced by firsthand investigations. Literacy and the processes of inquiry were symbiotic, each nurturing and sustaining the other. The more the children noticed about the moon through careful observations in their nightly moon journals, the more the content mattered. The more they conducted experiments (learning about oxygen in the Earth's atmosphere, making clouds, cleaning old rusty objects to hypothesize that both oxygen and water were on Mars at one time, creating moon craters with plaster of paris to understand how the surface of the moon came to be), the more they read to make connections and answer their questions. The nightly moon journal observations brought everything to life in clear and compelling ways.

Morning Meeting: Sharing Individual Moon Journals

Susan actually launched and sustained the energy of this unit during morning meeting. To inspire her six year olds to begin gazing into the heavens, Susan first shared entries from her own moon journal (which she began after visiting the Mauna Kea summit on the big island of Hawaii, home of one of the largest and most impressive telescopes in the world). After a week or so, she read nonfiction books and poetry about the moon to provide background that the students needed to pose solid, rather than surface-level, questions. She took the time to nurture initial understandings. Then she invited students to embark on the unit by having them begin their own moon journals. They shared them daily during the "share and news" component of morning meeting.

Susan described the way she implemented moon journals this way:

> The students kept moon journals for a full month and shared them every morning during morning meeting. The students observed the night sky (with special emphasis on the moon) and documented their observations. Some observations included the shape (phase), colors, and shading of the moon; number, color, and location of stars in the sky; and any constellations noted. Other observations included the temperature, wind speed, precipitation, and any other things of beauty or interest to the students. During the first few days, all students shared their journals with the class. After that, students pair/shared their journals, and then a student's name was pulled from a cup to share with the class. The selected student added his/her sketch and description to our class archive of the phases of the moon. I took pictures of the moon every night to correlate the photographs with the sketches.

Susan made sure that the form of the materials she used supported the function. For example, they decided to use lined paper on the left side of the moon journal for written observations and black construction paper on the right for sketches done in white crayons or chalk (see Figure 7.8). She also taught the children to make careful observations using binoculars.

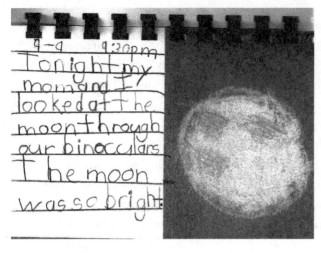

Figure 7.8a
Tonight my mom and I looked at the moon through our binoculars. The moon was so bright.

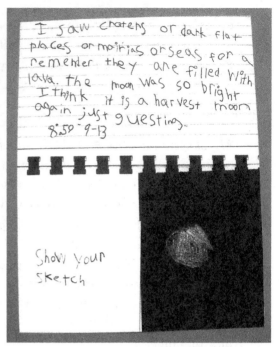

Figure 7.8b
I saw craters or dark flat places or [illegible] or seas. For a reminder they are filled with lava. The moon was so bright I think it is a harvest moon. Again, just guessing.

As the children began sharing their moon journal entries during morning meetings, Susan noticed they were composing substantive entries containing precise content information. She showcased the work of students who explained their observations using information from class science experiments or the texts they read, and others naturally followed suit. They learned the value of making educated guesses or predicting and became comfortable trying new ideas because they knew it was okay to take a risk to generate or revise a hypothesis.

Susan often shared her own moon journal entries, making her thinking and decisions explicit. When she was inspired to use a feature from a text they had read together, she told them where she got the idea. Of course, they followed her lead. Before long, many children began incorporating nonfiction text features into their moon journal observations. They became fond of sharing "fast facts" modeled in one of their favorite space books (see Figure 7.9).

The students began each day during this inquiry by reflecting on what they had noticed and wondered about in their moon journals.

10-5   7:45 PM
The moon is a little more than
half. fast fact: The moon has craters
Because asteroids, comicks and meteorites
hit The moon Because The moon Doesn't
have any armaster To protect it.

Figure 7.9
The moon is a little more than half. Fast fact: The moon has craters
because asteroids, comets, and meteorites hit the moon because the
moon doesn't have any atmosphere to protect it.

▶ Observe a Classroom Demonstration

VIDEO CLIP 4 demonstrates the ritual Susan established for sharing moon journal
entries. Students tell the time, date, and moon phase; then they add personal or
descriptive information. As you watch the video, follow along on the following transcript. Notice how these young astronomers practice the five processes of inquiry
featured in this book. They (1) make careful observations using the tools of the
discipline, (2) use the language of inquiry, (3) ask questions, (4) use primary and
secondary sources, and (5) reflect. Also notice how they work together as a community.

Joshua: 9:01. 10-5-11. I saw the moon. It was a waxing gibbous. It was
bright. It had a rainbow around it. It was beautiful. This is my sketch.
Carlin.

Carlin: Thanks, Joshua. 10-5-11. 9:29 PM. I went on the Internet. The webcast
we do is "Current Moon Sighting." It was a waxing gibbous. And it was
maybe 53 percent of full. I looked outside. The moon is twinkling like
a twinkling moon. This is my sketch. I didn't really get to draw it how
I wanted it to be. Kianna.

Kianna: Thank you, Carlin. 8:12 PM. Tonight the moon was so bright. It lit
up the sky like a flashlight.

Keaton: Sometimes I call it a secondary source. *(Keaton was referring to the
fact that he accessed the Internet to document the moon's phase. Susan had been
deliberately teaching them how to use primary and secondary sources through
the unit. Because Keaton couldn't sketch the actual moon the night before, he
used a secondary source to complete his moon journal entry.)*

Susan: It was a secondary source on the computer. So when you look at the moon with your eyes, what kind of a source is that? You guys?

Class: A primary source.

Susan: A primary source. But if you can't see the moon that night and you really want to know what it should look like, how do you find that out?

Class: Secondary source.

Susan: Secondary source. Okay, Goody.

Goody: The moon is almost a full moon.

Susan: Go ahead and read your poem. Do you want me to read your poem? Goody wrote a poem. And it says, "I love you, moon. We will see you in the morning." Okay, you guys. Since I have the mic, I'm going to share mine with you. "Wednesday, October 5th, 2011, 8:45 PM. The moon is a waxing gibbous and it is beautiful." And then I wrote, "Really exciting news!" And this was it. "As I was walking home from school last night, I saw a meteor streaking across the night sky. Space fact: A meteor is a meteoroid." Which is what, a rock or a small what?

Class: Asteroid.

Susan: Asteroid—that burns up as it passes through Earth's atmosphere. They are sometimes called shooting—

Class: Stars.

How Will Students Reflect on and Document Their Learning?

Clearly, writing workshop offered Susan ongoing opportunities to assess her young astronomers' growing understanding of content and nonfiction writing skills and strategies. In reality, our best evidence of student learning comes from naturally occurring data. If we take the time to analyze authentic classroom interactions and student artifacts using an assessment lens, we can track children's growth and change across the unit. In Susan's case, she documented a range of opportunities she would offer students to help them reflect on and document their own learning. As a teacher, she viewed genuine student artifacts as rich kid-watching data (Goodman 1978 and O'Keefe 2001). She used her unit plans for big picture thinking and ongoing kid-watching data to teach responsively day in and day out. The following list shows how Susan relied heavily on children's talk, writing, and sketching to interpret their learning, allowing her students to grow and change as readers, writers, and astronomers.

- We revisit our graffiti boards to see how many of our original questions are now answered and what we still want to explore.
- We review the sketches of the night sky and the moon.
- We share and discuss our moon journals.
- We write responses to books we have read.
- We have written conversations with each other and with our parents about the things we are learning.
- We share the notes we have taken after reading informational texts.
- We create a board of "wondrous words" as we "journey through space." I ask the children to help write definitions and illustrate the word cards.
- We write in different genres as we engage in the study of astronomy. For example, it is my hope that some of the students may want to write a poem, a song, or a fiction or nonfiction piece related to the things they are experiencing and learning.
- We have a class discussion after our evening of stargazing.
- We write individual thank you notes to our guest astronomer and include at least one thing that we learned from him.
- We share the things we learned during our Friday learning celebration.
- Hopefully the children will want to engage in some sort of project to help people who are still suffering from the effects of an earthquake (in Haiti, Chile, or elsewhere).

Next, they turned their attention to studying the geology of the Earth after studying other planets.

The Unit at a Glance

It's impossible to adequately capture a month's worth of dynamic teaching and learning around a topic as compelling as astronomy. In this chapter, Susan Bolte and I highlighted critical moments that made a genuine difference in her children's content and literacy learning. We shared the big picture vision she created in her unit plans and then contextualized the moments that mattered most within the curricular structures of morning meeting, reading, writing, and science workshops. To fully appreciate the depth and breadth of Susan's planning, see her unit of study, "Unit 2: Astronomy, Grade 1" in the online teaching resources. To better understand how to write a unit of study that includes the components featured in this chapter, and much more, see "Narrative 3: Planning Units of Study: Using a Unit Template."

I will always be grateful for the chance to live and learn alongside Susan Bolte and her first graders as they explored the universe. I was changed by the experience and hope your vicarious experience of it inspired and informed you. Susan and her students offered us a glimpse of curricular heaven. And it was good.

Online Teaching Resources

www.heinemann.com/products/E04603.aspx
Unit of Study Planning Template
Unit 2: Astronomy, Grade 1
Narrative 3: Planning Units of Study: Using a Unit Template
Video Clip 4: Moon Journals, Grade 1

Chapter 8

Across the Day and Year

Balancing Daily Planning with Long-Range Planning

There is such a thing as over-planning. We don't want to plan in a way that doesn't allow us to be responsive to our students and their needs. There's also such a thing as under-planning. If everything is improvised, it's too easy to miss out on a trajectory of growth from day to day and across the year. So what does "just-right" planning look like? It's a balance between the two. There are steps you can take ahead of time that will actually lift your capacity to be responsive in the moment later on. The better you plan, the more responsive you can be. And because most districts require teachers to create and submit long-range plans to start the year, that's a great place to begin.

QUESTIONS TO CONSIDER WHEN BEGINNING YOUR PLANNING

- What are the essential science and social studies concepts in your standards?
- What professions use them in real life? What tools and strategies do these professions use?

- What kinds of experiences might you provide in the classroom that mirror learning in the field?
- What kinds of high-quality nonfiction reading and writing experiences might be embedded authentically into units of study in science and social studies?

Planning by Alternating Units of Study in Science and Social Studies

Years ago Don Graves described the hectic rhythm of elementary classrooms as the "cha, cha, cha, curriculum." At the end of the day, we often feel exhausted and unfulfilled, as if we've danced on top of the curriculum with a little bit of this and a little bit of that. If we want to slow our teaching down enough to allow children to go deep, to truly learn how to think, work, and communicate, we need to rethink how we use time. Instead of trying to teach significant units of study in science and social studies concurrently (even though interdisciplinary ties can be made, of course), we have found it cleaner and more efficient to alternate the units.

As you are sketching out your long-range plans, consider how you might devote a few weeks to working as scientists, transition to working as historians, and then back to working as scientists. Figure 8.1 shows two schedules that contrast what is typically done in the name of long-range planning and what is possible when teachers alternate units of study in the sciences and social sciences.

Typical Long-Range Planning Schedule for Science and Social Studies in Third Grade, Both Subjects Taught Daily

Aug.–Sept.	Oct.–Nov.	Dec.–Jan.	Feb.–March	April–May
Landforms and bodies of water	Rocks and minerals	Plants and animals	Matter	Force/motion/ sound
Places, regions, social classes/ human systems in South Carolina	First Carolinians	Explorers	American Revolution	Social, Civil War/ Reconstruction

Figure 8.1

continues

Rotational Planning Schedule for Exploring the World as Scientists and Social Scientists in Third Grade

Aug.–Sept.	Oct.–Nov.	Dec.–Jan.	Feb.–March	April–May
Working as geologists	Exploring South Carolina as anthropologists and geographers	Learning as botanists and biologists	Historians investigate explorers, American Revolution, Civil War, and Reconstruction	Working as Chemists/ Physicists

Figure 8.1 continued

The Rhythm of Your Day: The Power of Daily Forecasts

Once you have a solid vision of the sequence of your year, you can zoom in on the flow of your day. Daily forecasts frame the curricular structures students can count on: time to explore; to converse during morning meetings; to think, work, and communicate as readers, writers, and mathematicians; and to delve deeply into a unit of study as scientists or social scientists. Daily forecasts also offer you the chance to plan for responsive teaching. By uniting your big picture vision and your students' current needs and interests, it is easier to make daily instructional decisions.

Curricular Structures That Support Inquiry

To make inquiry work, it has to be a part of daily classroom life. We create the habits of inquiry through curricular structures that support inquiry. In this chapter, you'll learn what those structures are, and why and how they support inquiry. Remember, inquiry is a stance. Students need lots of experience with it, so we need to offer them a variety of opportunities throughout the day. Specific curricular structures offer different opportunities for teaching and learning. Some promote learning about literacy, while others feature opportunities to learn through literacy. At CFI, we use a *daily forecast* that always includes the curricular structures shown in Figure 8.2. Like everything else in life, it's easier to commit to making something happen if we plan for it.

> **Curricular Structures That Happen Each Day to Promote Balanced Literacy**
>
> - Exploration (settling in)
> - Morning meeting (building community and curriculum)
> - Workshop (reading, writing, math)
> - Inquiry units (social studies and science)

Figure 8.2 The Daily Forecast

A schedule creates consistent, predictable habits. When classroom life is predictable, students devote their time and energy to accomplishing the task at hand rather than trying to understand what they are supposed to do or why. We want students to understand that this time is purposeful, that the work they're doing is worthy, and that they have agency within this structured time. Predictable structures across content areas help students focus on learning, enhance classroom community, and reduce classroom management dilemmas. As Lucy Calkins (2010) explains:

> *If the writing workshop is always changing, always haphazard, children remain pawns waiting for their teacher's agenda. For this reason and others, I think it is so important for each day's workshop to have a clear, simple structure. Children should know what to expect. This allows them to carry on; it frees the teacher from choreographing activities and allows time for listening. How we structure the workshop is less important than that we structure it.*

Because we want to foster in our students the learning and working habits of writers, readers, mathematicians, scientists, and social scientists, we follow the workshop structure across content areas that is shown in Figure 8.3.

> - *Demonstration:* using strategy lessons or minilessons to show students how and why
> - *Engagement:* living the process
> - *Reflection:* reflecting as individuals and/or groups on the content, skills, strategies, and concepts
> - *Celebration:* publicly recognizing growth and change

Figure 8.3 Workshop Structure

Each day, our students know they'll get a *demonstration* of new skills or strategies they might explore, think about, or try during the workshop. They know they will have the chance to *engage* in the authentic process of readers, writers, mathematicians, scientists, or social scientists. They know that it's important to *reflect* on strategies they employed during the workshop: to look back on what worked and what needs improvement, what they tried, and what risks they might take in the future. They also know they will be able to *celebrate* their growth and accomplishments by publishing their work, giving a presentation, sharing a science experiment in class or at a school share fair, participating in a student-led conference, and so on.

It's critical to promote an inquiry stance across curricular structures. Because such fine work has been done around reading, writing, and math workshops over the years, in this chapter I will feature the teaching and learning potential of (1) exploration, (2) morning meeting, and (3) integrated units of study in the sciences and social sciences. They offer ongoing opportunities to teach the skillfulness of inquiry and provide natural contexts for content literacy. The processes of inquiry featured in chapters 2 through 6 come to life daily through these curricular structures.

Exploration

Exploration is a curricular structure that offers students time every day to work on projects of their choice. Although some early childhood teachers find the period following lunch the best time for exploration, most teachers include exploration as their opening curricular structure. Because there is often a significant time lapse between the arrival of the first and last child each morning, devoting the first half hour to exploration gives teachers a chance to touch base with each child and gives kids a chance to work independently or in small groups until everyone arrives. It's a calm, productive way to start the day.

Exploration typically includes ongoing choices for students. Tim O'Keefe describes exploration this way: "Children may read independently or together, work on pieces they are preparing for publication, play chess or commercial games, make observations in the science area, read the local newspaper, write observations or questions in the class science, math, language, or news journal" (Mills, O'Keefe, and Jennings 2004, 15).

Teachers and students also devise exploration activities together in relation to their current unit of study. They might construct a geodesic dome out of chickpeas and toothpicks to connect with the geometry they are exploring in math workshop. They might have a station with batteries and bulbs to build circuits to further investigate ideas generated during their study of electricity. They might work as a small group to compose a song related to a topic they are investigating in social studies. (See the online teaching resources for Chapter 9 for a song about Rosa Parks.)

We make decisions about appropriate exploration choices based on their students' ages, their interests, and the issues they are pursuing as a community. Scott Johnson's fourth and fifth graders love exploring how things work, so he brings in old appliances for kids to take apart, figure out, and then reassemble. Although early childhood teachers often use technology to give kids a chance to read and listen to stories read orally or view live zoo cameras during exploration, intermediate teachers often make laptops available for kids to pursue personal inquiries online. (See "Narrative 5: Explanation and Demonstration of Exploration and Morning Meeting, Grade 2" in the online teaching resources.)

To be successful, we scaffold students into individual activities by introducing and practicing them as a class. It's not enough to simply offer diverse materials for students to explore. When children understand how to use a strategy or material, it is added to the class list of exploration choices. For instance, Tim teaches his second and third graders how to play chess because it demonstrates the importance of developing strategies and promotes good sportsmanship. Chess becomes an official exploration choice once Tim is confident his students understand the basics of playing the game.

Class Journals: Recording Lines of Inquiry

Class journals promote living as inquirers. Kids view the world through different lenses by documenting what they notice and wonder about. The journals are large booklets of tag board in which students write or sketch their connections or wonderings as readers, writers, mathematicians, scientists, or social scientists. In the beginning Tim helps them decide where entries should go. ("That sounds like you are wondering about a cultural practice, so put that in the culture journal." "That's the kind of question a mathematician might ask, so it would fit best in the math journal.") Soon they know exactly where to place an idea or question. There are times when an entry could comfortably fit in a couple of journals, demonstrating the integrated nature of life and learning.

Teachers contribute to the class journals as well, shaping children's thinking while planting seeds for future units of study. Insights and questions like those shown in Figure 8.4 inspire interesting conversations during morning meetings. The author of each entry typically calls on three friends to respond to keep the conversation moving.

Figure 8.4a Science Journal Entries

Relationship!!! My cat, rabbit, hamster, bird and fish act weird about being together around me and around them (each other). Why? Predators! My hamster hides, my bird flies and chirps. My fish glides quickly like he's scared. My rabbit hops scaredly. My cat hunches her back and pounces and meows and purrs! Why? Because the cat is a predator. Huh! Why? —Hunter Hayes

Joe and I found a turtle at his house on Saturday. (caption) Female yellow belly slider. —Martin/Joseph

I, Daquan Wise, have made two circuits with one battery. —Daquan

I have some of these beetles that I always find. —Sydney

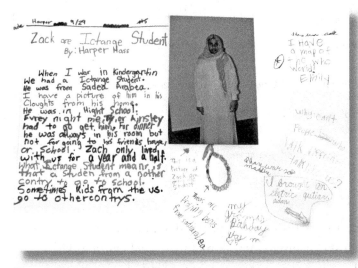

Figure 8.4b Culture Journal Entries

Zack our Exchange Student
By: Harper Hass
When I was in kindergarten we had an exchange student. He was from Saudi Arabia. I have a picture of him in his clothes from his home. He was in high school. Every night me or Ainsley had to go get him for dinner. He was always in his room but not for going to his friends' house or school. Zach only lived with us for a year and a half. What exchange student means is that a student [comes] from another country to go to school. Sometimes kids from the US go to other countries.

[on the right]

This is a picture of Zack our exchange student. These are praying beads from Saudi Arabia. —Harper

I have a map of the whole world. —Emily

Why can't people who talk different, talk like us?

I brought an electric guitar. —Aidan

My grandma's birthday was Monday. 75.

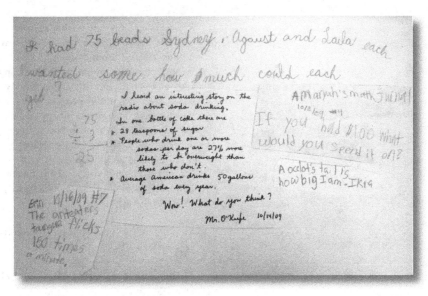

Figure 8.4c Math Journal Entries

I had 75 beads. Sydney, August and Laila each wanted some. How much could each get?

75 / 3 = 25

The anteater's tongue flicks 150 times a minute. —Erin

I heard an interesting story on the radio about soda drinking. In one bottle of Coke there are 28 teaspoons of sugar.

   People who drink one or more sodas a day are 27% more likely to be overweight than those who don't.
   Average American drinks 50 gallons of soda per year.
   Wow! What do you think? —Mr. O'Keefe

Amaryah's math journal. If you had $100 what would you spend it on?

A ocelot's tail is how big I am. —Ikia

   Class journals encourage kids to live with a sense of wonder, and to notice and name the world using different lenses or disciplines. Sometimes teachers help kids find answers or fine-tune their thinking; other times teachers and kids simply post and explore a new idea that matters to them. It's important to make space in the day for kids to share so that they can keep the journals fresh and alive. Students who complete an entry are assured the opportunity to share during morning meeting. When kids know they have to complete an entry to guarantee a spot in the conversation, they invest in the process and it becomes generative. They notice, name, and wonder about the world in and outside school.

Morning Meeting

Morning meetings offer a natural context for teachers and kids to wonder together and foster community building by engaging in exploratory conversations around individual and shared topics. In Tim's room, the morning meeting is one of the richest and most intellectually stimulating times of the day. It's when children make connections between the content they have been exploring in school and their personal lives. They also use this time to institutionalize the processes and adopt the multiple perspectives that are at the heart of inquiry, making this time central to curricular integration (Mills, O'Keefe, and Jennings 2004).

Time is our most valuable resource and there never seems to be enough of it, so it's important to carefully orchestrate morning meetings. Conversations should be equitable and student directed as much as possible. We have learned to create routines and rituals so that kids come to the meetings prepared to share, and we teach kids how to respond to the content and one another. We've found it very helpful for kids to call on three of their friends to respond to an idea or question they raise. To ensure that all voices are heard we use a strategy called "fist and fingers." Kids begin the meeting by holding up a fist. Once they've shared, they hold up a finger if they want to respond. Kids look around the circle to call on all the fists first. Then they begin calling on those with the fewest fingers. In this way, kids own the exploratory conversation while hearing diverse voices and perspectives on the topics they raise in class journals or about the news. This student-directed interaction pattern gives teachers the chance to focus on taking careful kid-watching notes along the way.

Many teachers invite kids to open morning meetings by sharing the news and entries from their class journals. Brief exploratory conversations follow each contribution. Teachers and kids ponder a range of topics from diverse perspectives and chart possible entries for inspiration. For example, Chris Hass's third graders generated ideas for math journal entries, as shown in Figure 8.5.

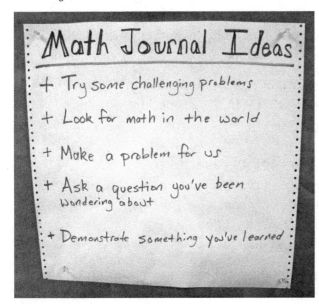

Figure 8.5 Math Journal Ideas

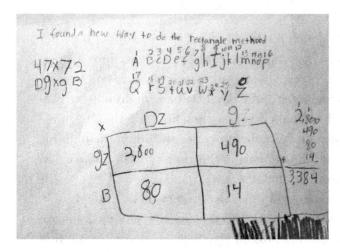

Figure 8.6 A New Way to Multiply

The journal entries become more sophisticated over time. One day a group of Tameka Breland's fourth graders shared and discussed a new way to multiply using the rectangle method. Tameka celebrated by posting the entry and leading the class to a new strategy for understanding, as shown in Figure 8.6.

Children also share current local, national, and international news by reading the local paper or logging on to an Internet children's news site. In fact, parents of CFI students have expressed their astonishment when their kids join them in reading the newspaper on Sunday mornings.

To foster ongoing inquiry into mathematics, many teachers lead exploratory conversations centered on the number of days the students have been in school: "What do you notice about [*the day number*]?" If this practice is ingrained, the children come to school prepared—they challenge themselves and one another to make new mathematical connections.

Charting the children's observations helps them use and build on previous contributions and documents students' learning over time. On day 74 in Michelle Kimpson's first-grade classroom, the kids generated multiple ways to make 74 (see Figure 8.7):

- counting money: 2 quarters, 2 dimes, and four pennies = 74 cents
- counting by fives using tally marks (5, 10, 15, 20, 25, 30, 35, 40, 45, 50, 55, 60, 65, 70) then adding 4 ones
- 70 + 4 = 74
- counting by tens: 10 + 10 + 10 + 10 + 10 + 10 + 10 + 4 = 74
- $(7 \times 10) + 4 = 74$ (They learned to recognize that multiplication is repeated addition: 7 tens plus 4 ones equals seventy-four)
- representing 74 with Roman numerals (LXXIV = 74)
- time: 74 minutes = 1 hour and 14 minutes

These young mathematicians began the year by discussing whether the number of the day was odd or even, counting by ones and then by fives, and making personal connections, like "My brother is eight years old," on the eighth day of school. By day

74 they had developed a range of strategies for posing and solving mathematical problems.

Many teachers open with a discussion of the daily weather forecast and prompt students to collect and interpret quantitative climate data. Children document temperature data on line graphs and compare data over time. They might track high

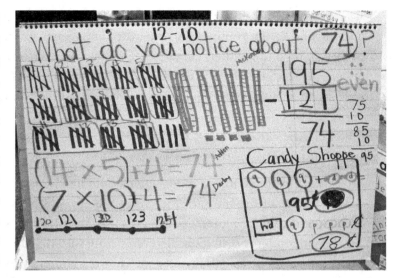

Figure 8.7

and low temperatures for 180 days and compare them with normal temperatures for the area (see Figure 8.8). Or, they might compare current trends to historical data to interpret climate change for themselves. In Tim O'Keefe's math workshop, monthly weather data collected across the year is used to teach students how to calculate mean, median, and mode. By making weather and climate data collection a morning meeting ritual, kids learn about mathematics and how to learn through mathematics.

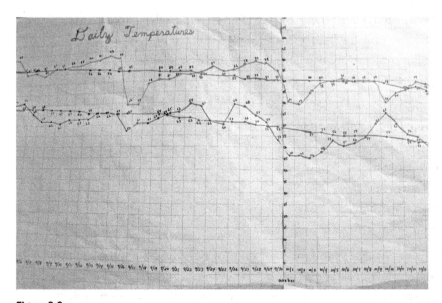

Figure 8.8

Morning meetings needn't (and shouldn't) be rigid and formulaic. Teachers and kids make the routines and rituals of class journals, daily news, mathematical observations, and weather/climate data their own, in their own ways. These predictable structures give kids the comfort (and inspiration) of knowing they will be able to share their insights and questions or make personal connections.

▶ *A Look Inside the Classroom:* Exploration and Morning Meeting

To see what exploration and morning meetings look, sound, and feel like, **VIEW VIDEO CLIP 5** and read the transcript of Tim O'Keefe and his second graders (see www .heinemann.com/products/E04603.aspx). Both curricular structures come to life as the second graders begin their day connecting with one another, with Tim, and with projects they are personally invested in. They read independently or together, work on pieces they are preparing for publication, play chess or other games, conduct science experiments, read the local newspaper, and write observations or pose questions in one of the class journals. Tim often helps a small group of children compose a song or conduct a science experiment. In this clip, Tim and a small group of children reconstruct the skeleton of a dead bat they had buried five months earlier. Here are a few things to notice:

- ▷ The other kids in the class are playing chess, reading, or writing in the background.
- ▷ Tim and the children in the group exchange exploratory comments and questions, moving fluidly in and out of mentor and apprentice roles and naturally using the language of inquiry:

  "I noticed . . ."
  "I wonder . . ."
  "I made a connection . . ."
  "I appreciated . . ."
  "I have a feeling . . ."
  "I was surprised by . . ."
  "This reminds me of . . ."
  "Building on . . ."

- ▷ They consult William as the resident mentor because he completed an impressive expert project on bats in first grade.
- ▷ They use nature magazines and the Internet to explore their emerging questions.

▶ They use primary and secondary sources to investigate and reconstruct the bat skeleton.

▶ Individual insights become part of the collective thought.

The transcript that follows is part of their conversation (the full transcript is online in "Narrative 5: Explanation and Demonstration of Exploration and Morning Meeting, Grade 2"). Notice the talk that nurtures the investigation: Tim leads from behind by talking scientist to scientist, teaching into and out of his students' connections and questions.

Tucker: There's another leg bone right about there, 'cause look (points to the model in the Zoobook).

Tim: Oh, I think we had that right. You're right, there are two leg bones together on the bottom.

Onastasia: We need to put these together.

Tim: So that's just like a human. There's one at the top, that's called the femur and there's two little ones down below.

Tucker: Look! It does go down there.

Tim: Ahh, but you know what? I have it reversed. No, that's right.

Carly (who joined the group out of curiosity): These must be the toes.

Tim: Yes, and you know those little tiny things? Lauren, you know those little tiny things that you found? I'll bet they're the claws.

Lauren: I'll bet the tinier ones are part of their tail spine.

Tim: Oh, you're right. No wonder they had such a long spine. I didn't even think about that. We had the ribs right too, I think.

Tucker: Yeah. They've got this one bone coming out of their ribs too. Kind of like right there [points to picture].

Tim: Let's see. And I think we're right about the big bones up here. Only the big bones [in the wings] kind of make a W or a V.

Tucker: Yeah, and the big bones go that way.

Tim: So if I put some glue—why don't you put some glue where you think these more slender bones go?

Onastasia: These? One of these?

Tim (pointing to the magazine): See how they come out sort of like a W from that point?

Onastasia: Oh, yeah.

Tim: Kind of like this maybe.

Carly (already gluing something): Excuse me, Onastasia—

Tim: Okay, wait, wait, wait, let's not do too much glue. You see how these bones are arranged in the picture?

Tucker: Mr. O?

Tim: Yes, Tucker?

Tucker: I'll bet you one of these bones goes right here because look, this is kind of right there under the center of those two bones.

Tim: It's kind of like our collar bone and our scapula, our shoulder bones.

Tucker: I broke my collar bone falling off a slide one day.

Tim: So which ones do you think might be the collar bones?

Integrated Units of Study in the Sciences and Social Sciences

Teachers at CFI create integrated units of study in the physical, biological, earth, and social sciences. They do so to uncover required content and standards in ways that reflect the holistic nature of knowledge and learning in the world. At the same time they strive to deliberately teach students how to use reading, writing, and mathematics as tools for learning. Communication systems and the disciplines are not isolated from one another in the world and they shouldn't be in the classroom. We highlight rather than isolate literacy strategies and content knowledge to help children understand their interrelated and interdependent nature. The following classroom examples illustrate how teachers bring integrated units in the sciences and social sciences to life . . . They show learning for real!

How an Embedded Inquiry Unfolds: Biology Unit, Grades 2 and 3

Tim and his second graders' reconstruction of the bat skeleton was not a random, isolated activity. It was part of a larger unit of study designed to help kids look at the world as biologists. When developing a vision for the unit (see Figure 8.9), Tim planned how he would help his children learn to work as biologists, not simply learn about biology. Because Tim teaches the same group of students for two years, he focused on observation, sketching, and questioning in second grade; then in third grade, he focused on reading and writing nonfiction about an animal they could directly observe.

In Second Grade

Tim used sketching to convey the importance of making careful observations from which to pose and investigate questions. He passed out blank paper and invited the children to draw a cricket. Most of the kids approached the task confidently. Next, Tim placed a cricket in a baby food jar in the center of each table. Students used

Biology Inquiry Unit

Much of the focus of this inquiry will be on observation and sharing insights and information. Personal experiences and anecdotes will be considered as important as information learned from outside sources.

We will conduct continuous observations of the natural world as well as up-close investigations of certain species. We will dissect owl pellets as a class to foster how to pose questions from careful observations. Through intensive investigations of particular species, children will learn what kinds of questions to ask about the animals they choose to study.

Direct observation of real animals will be one of the main methods of investigation. Animals may be observed in the school neighborhood as well as at home. Animals may be brought into the classroom for careful observation, note taking, and sketching. Zoo cameras and nature films will be used to observe and document animal behavior in a more or less natural setting.

Surveys may also contribute to knowledge of local animal populations. Tallying bird sightings at a bird feeder or ants on the playground are examples. We will investigate citizen science opportunities like Project Squirrel, Bat Detective, Big Butterfly Count, and the Great Sunflower Count.

In writing workshop we will focus on nonfiction writing using *Ranger Rick* magazines for inspiration. The children will learn to read like nonfiction nature writers by writing expert project pieces about an animal they have observed over time. Once they have collected extensive observation data, they will pose questions and read to investigate the creature of their choice. The children will write a *Ranger Rick*–like piece about an animal they have directly observed and researched, using primary and secondary sources.

Children will be asked to learn in-depth information about a single animal and to share that information with the rest of the class and school through expert project presentations. Their piece about the animal of their choice will be the written component of their expert project. Criteria for the projects will be constructed as a class and reflect the language and content of biology.

Interviews with local naturalists as well as the professionals at the local zoo will add a professional perspective.

  —Tim O'Keefe

Figure 8.9

magnifying glasses to compare their initial sketches with the specimen. Then they carefully sketched the cricket while looking through a magnifying glass. As they sketched, they talked about what they noticed. They realized that their initial drawings resembled a cartoon, and the sketches they completed with the support of a primary source looked like those in nature magazines or field guides. The closer they looked, the more they wondered about the function of each insect part.

Tim asked the group to reflect throughout the process: "Hey, boys and girls. A lot of kids are noticing things that you can't exactly capture in your drawing, like one of these crickets seems to be sort of wiping its antennae with its front legs. I'd say go ahead and use words, too. So sketch and then also write about the behavior that you see. Another thing: You may want to draw these animals from different angles. Like Brandon is going to draw one from the side, but he said, 'Their wings are kind of over-lapping, I noticed that.' You might want to draw a top view in order to catch that part of your observation. So sketch and write on the bottom about their behavior, okay?"

Because science workshop follows the same predictable pattern as other work-shops (demonstration, engagement, reflection, and celebration), the second graders gathered to reflect on what they learned through sketching their observations (see Figure 8.10). Tim began by saying, "Before I looked at a cricket up close, I had all kinds of wrong impressions about what their bodies were like. One was—and I noticed

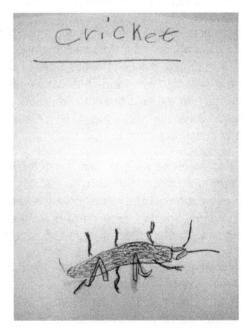

Figure 8.10 Before   After

this on a lot of people's drawings—where their antennae are placed. Their antennae come out of the front of their heads. And I noticed a lot of you, even when you were looking at a cricket, put their antennae on the back of their heads. And so I still think that you're kind of going from the impressions you had before. But as we learn more about crickets, especially by observing them and looking at their body parts and stuff, your second drawings, or even your third or fourth drawings—probably each one is going to get a little bit closer to the way they actually look. Same thing about the way their legs are coming out. Most kids knew, after they observed a cricket, that they have six legs. But look carefully tomorrow when we look at these—where are the legs coming out of the body? They don't come out all over. A lot of kids kind of put their legs like this you know, six legs like this [*uses his fingers to demonstrate six legs in a straight row*]. But if you look carefully at those crickets, that's not really how their legs come out at all. So tomorrow as we get back to these, we will think together about every structure. Think about its head. Think about its wings. Think about the big legs and the small legs. We'll do some reading about crickets tomorrow too."

In Third Grade
Students built on this foundation by carefully observing, sketching, and discussing insights and questions about particular animals. After studying one animal together in depth, these young biologists generated a list of the characteristics they had noticed. Then, in small groups, they investigated different animal classifications—mammals, reptiles, amphibians, and so on. Each group generated a thorough list of characteristics exhibited by each species. They also identified the function of each characteristic. They addressed what, why, and how in relation to each animal group.

Next, Tim taught the children how to read nonfiction as writers and use what they learned to write a magazine article about an animal of their choice. They were free to investigate and write about an animal they were personally interested in, but it had to be one they could directly observe in their own backyard or neighborhood or via a webcam. For a week's homework they carefully documented their observations of the animal's behavior and related information, such as its habitat. They used graphs, charts, sketches, and narratives to capture their observations.

Only then did they turn to secondary sources related to their animal. They read voraciously because they were intrigued. They posed genuine questions because they really wanted to know. As they read, many of their observations made more sense to them. The more you know someone or something, the more you care. And the more you care, the more the reading matters. They read and they read and they read, taking notes along the way.

After taking notes on primary and secondary sources, Tim and his students read several *Ranger Rick* articles together, pausing to notice and name the moves the authors made that were especially powerful. They charted what they noticed, as shown in Figure 8.11.

Nonfiction Text Features in *Ranger Rick* Articles

- Pictures have captions.
- There are strong creative introductions, even for each header (questions, dares, amazing information up front).
- Headers let you know what is coming up—and serve as a tool for organizing ideas.
- There are creative titles with subtitles (primary and secondary headers).
- The writer makes you care about the animal.
- The pictures really go with the words.
- Paragraphs are used to organize smaller chunks of information.
- Fun invitations encourage you to read on ("let's pounce to the next page").
- Information is presented in a logical order or sequence.
- There is descriptive, clear language and interesting word choice.
- Some of the stories are written from a first person ("first animal") point of view.
- Question/answer format is used effectively.
- Each begins with a question.
- Quotation marks are used around things they "think" are true.
- Math is used to make things easy to understand.
- Bold letters and different fonts are used for emphasis.

Figure 8.11

Finally, the students pulled everything together by writing an article about their animal. Tim told them to use the list they had created for inspiration and direction. They decided to incorporate five of these characteristics in their pieces, individually deciding which ones they wanted to try. Tim made copies of the list for each student, and they checked off their choices and highlighted their use of these characteristics in their rough drafts. As they were putting the finishing touches on their rough drafts, Tim conferred with his young authors:

Tim: So, what did you guys think about those text features from that *Ranger Rick* magazine? And that whole thing that we did of reading all those and creating that list—what do you think about that list? Does it work for you? Does that seem helpful at all?

Simon: It does work for me.

Tim: Can you say more about it? Why was it helpful?

Simon: Well, last year I just wrote things like fact after fact after fact. And this year I'm writing more things like, "Have you ever been to the Blue Ridge Mountains? If you have and you saw the leaves rustle and little yellow eyes pop out, you probably saw an American toad."

Tim: And doesn't that sound just like something you might read in a professional article written for *Ranger Rick*? How about some of the rest of you? How has this list maybe helped you craft your writing?

Brandon: Just like Simon, last year I just wrote fact after fact after fact. Now, when it said on the Ranger Rick nonfiction text features [*reading from his list*], "The writer makes you care about the animal," I looked at that one and tried to make the reader feel about my animal so I added something at the end. And it's in my predators group, and it says—

Tim: Remind us what your animal is.

Brandon: My animal is the green anole. [*Reading from his draft*] "Predators: Snakes and birds, we are predators to a lot of animals just like these anoles. Did you know that more people kill more green anoles than their real predators? Always remember that if you catch any green anoles please feed them and then release them. These are really fascinating reptiles. These reptiles are really lucky that they are not in captivity.

Tim: So, one of the things that I love about that little section of your piece is, I know you didn't read that somewhere. That's something that really came right out of your heart. And it just seems to me that the most well crafted writing really comes from something that you truly care about. That's one of the most difficult features to get—to make the reader care about your animals.

As Tim conferred with his young authors, they articulated the composing moves they had made as nonfiction authors. They also revealed how they incorporated accurate content information from their primary and secondary sources. All five processes of inquiry were woven into this project seamlessly. This embedded inquiry gave these students a chance to live, learn, and communicate as biologists.

How an Embedded Inquiry Unfolds: Normalcy and World Cultures, Grade 2

When Chris Hass envisioned an inquiry into cultures for a unit of study in social studies, he saw it in the context of an investigation of normalcy. He deliberately planned to meet social studies and ELA standards and so much more. As his second graders read and wrote to learn about cultures around the world, they also developed a healthy skepticism toward their own and published knowledge of "others."

Chris first addressed normalcy, helping his students see the importance of understanding rather than judging others. He taught them to value diverse ways of being and to avoid stereotyping when learning about others. His plan for the inquiry is shown in Figure 8.12.

Inquiry into Normalcy and World Cultures

Hold class discussion around the questions "What does normal mean?" and "What is normal?" Follow up with a discussion of the term *abnormal*.

In small groups, have students create a mural of a "normal" second grader. Manipulate groupings so that some are homogeneous (gender, race) and others are heterogeneous. Groups will share their posters with the class and explain how they came to determine what to use as a representation of normal—particularly, how was this negotiated in mixed groups? Explore how this relates to notions of normalcy in our school, community, and world.

Read texts dealing with people being "othered." Titles may include *Chrysanthemum*, *One Green Apple*, *Cheyenne Again*, *Terrible Things*, and *Stand Tall, Molly Lou Melon*. During each read-aloud, support kids in conversations about normalcy and how it is used as a weapon against those who do not fit within this narrow definition.

Figure 8.12   *continues*

Introduce *Children of the World*. Take a picture walk through the book, noting the kids from each country. Discuss: Are people all the same? Why might some people say that people are all the same? What do they mean by this? In what ways are we different from one another? What is the place of difference in the world? How might some people react to difference? What can we do to counteract negative stereotypes?

Invite many classroom guests to talk about the cultures or groups with which they identify. Ask them to address negative stereotypes that exist about their culture or group, to include race, nationality, religion, health, and body type. Keep an ongoing class chart to record what we learn from each visitor. Have the kids keep notes and reflect after each visitor, adding to our "What We Know Now" list.

Create scenarios in which someone is being bullied, excluded, or teased based on a difference. Have kids, in small groups, develop varied strategies for dealing with each situation. How do we take action when we see something bad happening?

Watch "What Would You Do?" on You Tube (www.youtube.com/watch?v=G0D4_hFnRIU). This video deals with the mistreatment of a Muslim woman at a bakery. Discuss the people who spoke out against her as well as the many who just stood by and watched without taking action. Think about those who did take action: What did they do? What other choices were there for taking action? What would we do in such a situation?

Watch segments from the *Unwelcome in America* program on CNN (www.youtube.com/watch?v=gRlqz3e9OrA). Discuss what is happening and why. What questions do we have? How do we feel about this? What would we do in such a situation?

Launch a class study of China. Use this as an opportunity to address incorrect preconceptions, to highlight the similarities between Chinese and Americans, and delight in the differences. Address nonfiction reading, note-taking skills, determining importance, summarizing, using text and nontext features and so forth. Have the kids pool all their information onto posters with class-generated subtopics (schooling, homes, etc.). In small groups, have them organize the information and identify what questions are left unanswered. Find the answers to those questions. Have groups then take one subtopic and create a presentation that informs and intrigues. Follow this with a discussion about how researching another culture doesn't truly mean we understand them, but it's a good start. Conclude with a written reflection on why we learn about others. Use this to address any notions of a "Great White Hope."

Figure 8.12 continued

continues

Have the kids choose cultures of interest for individual study. This is an opportunity to share their family's culture, learn more about where their family came from, or explore a culture they know little about. At the conclusion of the study have kids share this with the school.

Identify ways other cultures are represented in picture books, television, and movies. In cases where this representation is insensitive, launch a letter-writing campaign.

Conclude with reflective discussion and writing around how this study has changed us. How will we live differently tomorrow than we did yesterday?

—Chris Hass

Figure 8.12 continued

Starting by Studying Themselves

First, Chris had the kids study themselves to get in touch with the notion of normalcy. He organized kids into homogeneous and heterogeneous groups based on gender and ethnicity, and then he asked them to create a mural that represented a typical second grader. Chris took careful notes as the kids constructed and reflected on the murals they created (see Figure 8.13). Then he helped them (1) recognize how they used the characteristics of the majority to determine what was normal, (2) critique who has the power to determine what is normal, and (3) ask themselves about fairness.

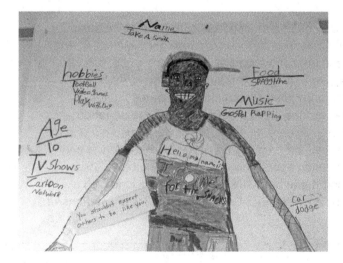

Figure 8.13

After they examined their decision-making process, they recognized how important it was to think deeply about what they considered normal, both individually and collectively. To take action on this new understanding, they codified words of wisdom or advice to keep in mind when learning about others:

- You shouldn't expect others to be like you.
- It's important to learn about others. This helps us avoid saying or believing things that are untrue or hurtful.
- There's no such thing as "normal."
- Some people use the idea of "normal" to hurt others. Our job is to stop this from happening. TAKE POSITIVE ACTION!

During an especially powerful conversation, Maisy made a comment that everyone quickly embraced. It became the big idea that framed their year together: *There's no such thing as normal, just different.*

Reading to Learn

Next, Chris turned to a powerful picture book to further interrogate the hazards of "othering" in the world. He introduced *Cheyenne Again*, by Eve Bunting (1995), this way:

> *This book is by an author we know really, really well, Eve Bunting. Think back on some books that we read by her:* The Wednesday Surprise, One Green Apple. *And remember* Sunshine Home, *about the little boy who went to the nursing home? This one is called* Cheyenne Again. *There you can see Eve Bunting's name. Oh, we also read* A Day's Work, *about the boy whose grandfather had just come from Mexico. And he got him a job but he did it wrong but they fixed it in the end.*
>
> Cheyenne Again *ties in with some things we are thinking about* Stone Fox *or learning in* Stone Fox. *It's tied in with these things we are thinking about culture, that there's no such thing as normal and that one culture isn't better than another, and we should understand people who are different and not treat them badly. But I also think it ties in with this idea that we have been looking at in the last couple of weeks that reading is thinking, and that when we read we get these really strong thoughts or reactions sometimes about things that we want to turn and talk to someone about.*

Then he read the book aloud, stopping now and then to give kids a chance to pause and ponder—to turn and talk with a partner and then share their thinking with the whole group.

Chris: Does somebody want to share a piece of their conversation? I love reading Eve Bunting's books because she always has something in there to talk about that's really, really important.

Tyler: I think that the school he went in looked pretty scary.

Chris: It looked like a scary place to you? Look at that picture. That's the power of an illustration, right? Absolutely. It doesn't look inviting.

Trent: Well that was just the sleeping room. It doesn't look happy.

Chris: It doesn't look happy, no. Erica what did you want to say?

Erica: Me, Grace, and Chase were talking, we agreed that if we were Native American we wouldn't want to be taken either like the boy, because he sounds pretty mean.

Chris: Well, let's find out what happens. [*He reads through the sentences "The Indian in us must disappear they say. It must be tamed."*]

Rachael: What's *tamed* mean?

Chris: What does *tamed* mean? Do you know Trent?

Trent: Take control of it.

Chris: To take control. And we use the word tamed when we are referring to something that is wild. Like you might tame a wild animal. You might make it under control. So if you use the word *tame* with a Native American, you're implying that Native Americans are wild, right? And you're trying to control them. That's a word with a lot of intention.

Rachael: That is very mean.

Chris: Maisy?

Maisy: On that page it kind of tells you Native Americans and Indians have very different beliefs than us.

Chris: How's that?

Maisy: Because it talks about how they go to church and they learn about, um, they must have different gods that they believe in.

Chris: Absolutely. And one of the reasons for people coming to this, to North America, originally was to escape a place where they said you had to belong to the same church. You had to be of the same religion. They were actually coming here so they could have that freedom. But then maybe once they got here some people tried to do that to other people. Right? To get them all to believe in the same religion. Why don't you turn and tell someone what you're thinking. There were a couple people who wanted to say things. [*The kids share their thinking with partners, then with the whole group. The conversation ends this way.*] (See Figure 8.14.)

Things We're Beginning to Discover About Culture

- When it comes to people, *there's no such thing as normal.*
- The word *normal* suggests that differences are bad. Differences are not bad. Differences are both natural and good.
- Some people use the idea of normal to hurt people who are different from them. They hurt them with their words and their actions. This is wrong!
- *It's important to learn about others.* This helps us avoid saying and believing things that are untrue or hurtful.

Figure 8.14

Studying One Culture as a Class

After Chris had established guidelines for avoiding stereotyping as much as possible, they began a whole-class inquiry into one country—China—so Chris could help them learn how to learn about others. As they worked with partners to understand China, they used sticky notes to document their learning. Chris created a folder with different categories to place-hold their ideas:

- I Think I Know . . .
- Yes! I Was right!
- New Facts
- I Wonder . . .
- I Was So Wrong!

These categories promoted inquiry and helped them get comfortable with the tentative nature of knowledge.

After completing their whole-class inquiry, the students invited a primary source, a visitor from China, to their classroom. They shared their research and invited her to respond. She confirmed many of their ideas and helped them revise or fine-tune others.

Finally, they embarked on their own individual inquiries, investigating a culture that was personally meaningful to them in some way. The children explored countries such as Cambodia, Israel, Tanzania, Ukraine, Sweden, and Germany, all cultures that were represented in the classroom. They found personal connections to other people and places through these projects, and they used the processes Chris had introduced in their whole-class inquiry into China.

As the kids pursued their personal inquiries, Chris invited primary sources to share their firsthand knowledge about cultures. Visitors helped the kids learn:

- About Somali-Bantu refugees who had resettled in Columbia, South Carolina.
- About life in Ecuador, Libya, Iceland, Sierra Leone, Germany, England, and South Africa.
- About dwarfism.
- That one individual can't speak for or represent an entire culture. (Tameka Breland told them, eloquently, "I can't tell you what African American culture means to everyone, but I can talk about what it means to me.")
- How Tanzanians carry their babies (see Figure 8.15).

Figure 8.15

They concluded the unit of study with expert project presentations to parents and the entire school in a "share fair."

Through this inquiry, the children learned how to learn while exploring diverse cultures around the world. Chris Hass reflected on the unit this way:

This inquiry went very well. The most powerful experiences were the opportunities to have visitors come in and talk about their home cultures of Libya, China, Ecuador, and Tanzania. We were also able to hear about African American culture, Muslim refugees, dwarfism, and secondhand accounts of South Africa and Iceland. Our final guest had many cultures within her family and helped us see that these are not simplistic labels we attach to people. We are touched by all our experiences. In this way culture becomes unique for each of us.

Although Chris' perspective matters tremendously, it was the children's spontaneous comments that revealed how the unit impacted them as learners and citizens of the world. One day a student made a comment about African music being abnormal, when Maisy retorted, "There's no such thing as normal, just different." Because of the thoughtful work they had been doing together, the class responded to Maisy positively, making her observation the big idea they revisited across the year.

I witnessed the impact of Chris' unit as a visitor reporting on my firsthand experiences with refugees as a sponsor of a Somali Bantu family. Because the family was Muslim, many of the kids' misconceptions and fears surfaced as I shared my stories. It didn't take long for the class to see their beauty and wisdom, and to appreciate the incredible hardships they encountered and overcame in a refugee camp before coming to America. As I was wrapping up our conversation Rachel commented, "I used to think [they] were dangerous, but that was before I knew. Now I know they're kind and have big hearts." As students acquired in-depth insights into cultures around the world, they also learned of the hazards of overgeneralizing, stereotyping, and "othering." Chris positioned his students to change their hearts, minds, and actions by exploring and encountering others. As they did, they brought the school's mission statement to life, taking responsibility for "developing ourselves as more thoughtful, caring, and intelligent people who delight in learning and are committed to creating a more compassionate, equitable, knowledgeable, and democratic world!"

Online Teaching Resources

www.heinemann.com/products/E04603.aspx

Narrative 4: Explanation and Photo Collage of Kindergarten Exploration

Narrative 5: Explanation and Demonstration of Exploration and Morning Meeting, Grade 2

Video Clip 5: Exploration and Morning Meeting, Grade 2

Unit 3: Biology, Grades 2 and 3

Unit 4: Normalcy/World Cultures, Grade 2

Chapter 9

In Their Own Words

Children Who Are Responsible, Joyful Learners

In the chapters and video clips you've seen, I focused on the moves teachers make. Now it's time to look at the outcome of this work: student ownership of learning and achievement. After all, what matters most is the lasting impact our teaching has on our students' lives. A few years ago Julie Waugh was concluding her first day with a new group of fourth graders. Caitlyn was new to Julie's class and to our school, so Julie made an effort to check in with her several times during the day. As Caitlyn was zipping her book bag getting ready to go home, Julie asked, "So how was your day?" Caitlyn's face lit up as she responded, "I feel smarter here."

Comments like this and others led Julie and me to ask her fifth graders to reflect on life and learning at CFI (Mills and Donnelly 2001). Here are some of their comments.

- "The kids are a part of the curriculum."
- "The teachers trust us enough to give us privileges that other schools don't have. Except we have to understand that there are responsibilities that go along with those privileges . . . Basically our school is held together by trust and love!!!"
- "Part of school is connections. That may be connections to our lives, other people, books, the past, or anything else. Connections are good

because they may break down anything we don't understand or may even help teachers determine whether you understand or not."

- "Here writing is like painting a picture with words. If you've ever read a good book, you know what I mean."
- "We value each other and our work."
- "We learn from our mistakes."

In the three video clips showcased in this chapter, you'll see children interpret their own learning. They show and tell how and why their learning evolved.

Teaching is a reciprocal relationship: We respond to invitations from our students, as when two fifth graders inspired their teacher, Julie Waugh, to launch an inquiry into magazines during writing workshop. And students respond to invitations from us, as when first graders seized the opportunity to make recommendations for cool projects they could add to Jennifer's plans when studying rocks and soil. Daquan and his third-grade friends built upon their teacher's invitation to create an expert project on heroes, which culminated a song to honor Rosa Parks, one that they composed and produced. You'll read more about these three examples in a few pages.

When you watch the clips, you'll see what happens when children are given opportunities to know and be known. In each case, what transpired exceeded the teachers' expectations of what was possible.

Teachers regularly ask themselves what is best for children. And we are at our best when we listen to children for the answers. This doesn't necessarily happen by asking children direct questions, but rather by listening for what they know, what they need to know, and what they are curious about.

First Unit of Study in First Grade: Inquiry into Rocks and Soil

> *The first graders are learning to work as scientists by exploring the wonders of dirt and soil.*
> —CARA, FIFTH GRADE

In video clip 6 we find Jennifer Barnes' and her first graders inquiring into rocks and soil on day 13 of the school year. As soon as I entered Jennifer's classroom, the children approached me with stories about their current unit of study on rocks and soil. I spontaneously asked Jennifer and her children to tell me about their work. As these charming children share their learning in unrehearsed ways, you get a clear glimpse of the responsive nature of Jennifer's teaching.

⊙ *A Look Inside the Classroom:* Inquiry into Rocks and Soil

AS YOU WATCH VIDEO CLIP 6 of Jennifer and her students as they explain their inquiry into rocks and soil, notice the intentional and systematic nature of Jennifer's moves and the ways she helps children make connections across curricular structures such as read-aloud, writing workshop, and their current unit of study. Notice, too, how she uses the tools and language of the various disciplines (geologist, petrologist, paleontologist) children are exploring. Children are learning how to be inspired by others while learning to make their strategies their own.

The children have choice and ownership in the content of their work as Jennifer shows them how to learn within and across curricular structures. She teaches them how to use tools such as goggles and magnifying glasses as they investigate rocks and soil samples they brought from home. They learn how to document their careful observations on the soil observation template. And they learn how to use primary and secondary sources in concert.

As Jennifer reflects on their past learning history, she provides a glimpse into their future. Jennifer teaches responsively by creating curriculum with and for children. She takes into account their insights and questions about the topic at hand as well as the children's strengths and needs as learners. In this case, their inquiry into rocks and soil will naturally transition into learning to think, work, and communicate as botanists. (See Jennifer's unit of study, "Unit 5: Rocks and Soil, Grade 1" in the online teaching resources.)

Student-Initiated Magazine Inquiry in Fifth Grade

> *"At school, everyone is a committed writer . . .*
> *It's part of our daily lives."*
> —DEANNA, FIFTH GRADE

Fourth- and fifth-grade teacher Julie Waugh inherited children who had been living and learning as authors with Jennifer Barnes and Tim O'Keefe from kindergarten through third grade. In fourth grade, Julie built on their past as writers by scaffolding them into publishing their work electronically. By the time children enter fourth and fifth grade they understand that authors need to read intensively and extensively within their genre. Listen in as two young authors reveal the ways they inspired their teacher to launch an inquiry into magazines. They understand the writing process from the inside out and convey the moves their teacher made to make the unit such a smashing success.

▶ *A Look Inside the Classroom:* Inquiry into Magazines

IN VIDEO CLIP 7 you'll notice that the girls have internalized the idea that they should look through magazines to get ideas before launching a magazine project. Their classroom teacher embraces an apprenticeship model, so they share their vision for the magazine project with her, knowing she will offer support as the mentor author/teacher in the classroom. These authors are so in touch with the process that they can explain Mrs. Waugh's teaching moves. For example: "We read *National Geographic Explorers* to really get us interested and write different kinds of articles—nonfiction, fiction, and contests."

Julie creates a unit of study around the magazines using both reading and writing workshop to strengthen children's inquiry into magazines. This project offers the students choice and ownership, giving them a chance to grow as writers while building on the identities they have constructed as learners over time. Some write historical pieces or sports stories; others write columns about things they love, like snake hunting or book reviews. At the time of the taping the girls are still looking for a "Dear Abby" kind of person.

Notice the strong sense of agency these girls exhibit from the project's inception. The girls keep track of their young colleagues' contributions and voluntarily work on the project at home as well as at school.

Although the girls are poised to move into the publication of their magazines, they haven't done so yet. When they do, Mrs. Waugh will conduct final editing conferences using the Adult Edit template she created. She will read and respond to each piece, and then she'll confer with each author, making notes regarding the conventions and word choices they are using. She will look for patterns in her data to construct minilessons for small groups and the whole class. She teaches individual authors during editing conferences and then teaches whole class and small group minilessons based on patterns of strengths and needs she identified during the conferences. (See Julie's unit of study on magazines in the online teaching resources.)

Inquiry into Song Writing: A Tribute to Rosa Parks

> *"It's difficult to imagine how hard it must have been*
> *To be treated so unfairly for the color of your skin*
> *Civil rights are so important—people must be free*
> *We're all created equal—it's so simple don't you see."*
> —Excerpt from song Tim O'Keefe's third graders
>   wrote entitled "From Slavery to Freedom"

Third-grade teacher Tim O'Keefe is a musician who composes songs, so he is able to teach his children how to capture important lessons learned and convey them through music. Kids are given opportunities to compose and perform songs written about topics they generate themselves. Although most songs are inspired by one student's ideas, individual insights become part of the class thought collective when composing songs; this in turn enhances the depth and breadth of their inquiries. The kids grow as writers by exploring how songs are constructed. They learn to read like writers when analyzing songs they love, to help them compose new ones. They find inspiration for songs in powerful children's literature, movies, units of study, and life experiences. Critical issues, such as teaching for social justice, are woven into the fabric of the curriculum, not simply addressed during a particular unit of study.

When Tim creates curriculum *with* and *for* his students they learn to ask, "So what?" and "Now what?" After his students completed their biography expert projects on someone who had changed the world, someone who made the world a better place, Daquan took these two questions to heart. He conducted his expert project presentation on Rosa Parks. He was so inspired by what he learned through his personal inquiry, he suggested they compose a class song in her honor.

⏵ *A Look Inside the Classroom:* From an Individual Biography to Class-composed Song for Rosa Parks

AS YOU VIEW VIDEO CLIP 8, you will notice the biography project uncovered the English Language Arts and Social Studies standards and so much more. For Tim it was part of a larger vision to promote a social action stance. When reading the lyrics, you will notice that Tim, Daquan, and friends did not settle for surface-level, romantic interpretations of why Rosa wanted to sit down on that historic day. There is a common, oversimplified misconception that Rosa simply had a "tiring" day and that is why she made the fateful decision not to move to the rear of the bus. In reality, Rosa was far from frail. She was a remarkably strong woman. She was a civil rights warrior. She was TIRED OF SEGREGATION . . . period. As Tim put it, "We investigated THE BIG TIRED."

Please read the lyrics as the kids sing the class song they composed. You'll see the depth and breadth of these third graders' understanding, passion, and compassion. You'll also notice that there is a significant shift in the last line of the chorus: Tim and his kids convey that they know there is still much work to be done. "WE WILL NOT GIVE UP OUR SEAT" means that the kids are invested in continuing the push for civil rights and social justice themselves. In fact, the kids sold CD's of their cover tunes (which included this song) to raise money for a charity entitled Rwandan HUGS.

They used the donations to purchase goats for Rwandan families—all as a tribute to a hero who truly made a difference in the world. (See Tim's unit of study, "Unit 7: Civil and Human Rights, Grade 3" in the online teaching resources.)

Jennifer, Julie, Tim, and their students all show what is possible when teachers and students engage in collaborative inquiry. May they inspire you and your students to live and learn together through inquiry.

ROSA PARKS

by Tim O'Keefe's Third Graders at the Center for Inquiry

Rosa Parks was tired of giving up her seat
Tired of separate lives and walking on the far side of the street
Rosa Parks was tired of working hard for low pay
Of saying "Yes, Sir" to the white man
Of separate parks for kids to play.
(Chorus)
Rosa was our hero
She would not give up her seat

She changed the world with her sacrifice
She would not give up her seat
She helped save us from prejudice
She would not give up her seat
Rosa was our hero
WE WILL NOT GIVE UP OUR SEAT.

Rosa Parks was tired of the man who wanted her seat
So she and her strong people walked hard in the cold and heat
Rosa parks was tired she tried to rest her feet
The bus filled up and the driver said,
"You must give up your seat!" **(Chorus)**
Rosa Parks was tired when she got on the bus
She paid her fare like she always did and she didn't make a fuss
Rosa Parks was tired but strong as she could be
And Montgomery worked together
To make the people free. **(Chorus)**
(Bridge)
All fair-minded people
Wanted integration
The boycott worked successfully
And defeated segregation. **(Chorus)**

Online Teaching Resources

www.heinemann.com/products/E04603.aspx
Video Clip 6: Inquiry into Rocks and Soil, Grade 1
Video Clip 7: Magazine Inquiry, Grade 5
Video Clip 8: Rosa Parks and Civil Rights, Grade 3
Unit 5: Rocks and Soil, Grade 1
Unit 6: Magazines, Grades 4 and 5
Unit 7: Civil and Human Rights, Grade 3

References

Calkins, Lucy. 2010. *Launch an Intermediate Writing Workshop: Getting Started with Units of Study for Teaching Writing, Grades 3–5*. Portsmouth, NH: Heinemann.

Goodman, Yetta. 1978. "Kidwatching: An Alternative to Testing." *National Elementary School Principal* 57(4): 41–45.

Halliday, M. A. K. 1975. *Learning How to Mean: Explorations in the Development of Language*. London: Edward Arnold.

Johnston, Peter H. 2004. *Choice Words: How Our Language Affects Children's Learning*. Portland, ME: Stenhouse.

———. 2012. *Opening Minds: Using Language to Change Lives*. Portland, ME: Stenhouse.

Lindfors, Judith Wells. 1999. *Children's Inquiry: Using Language to Make Sense of the World*. New York, NY: Teachers College Press.

Mills, Heidi, and Amy Donnelly, eds. 2001. *From the Ground Up: Creating a Culture of Inquiry*. Portsmouth, NH: Heinemann.

Mills, Heidi, Timothy O'Keefe, and Louise B. Jennings. 2004. *Looking Closely and Listening Carefully: Learning Literacy Through Inquiry*. Urbana, IL: National Council of Teachers of English.

Mills, Heidi, Timothy O'Keefe, and David Whitin. 1996. *Mathematics in the Making*. Portsmouth, NH: Heinemann.

Mills, Heidi (Guest Editor), Susi Long, and Franki Sibberson (Coeditors). 2005. "Assessment as Knowing and Being Known." *School Talk* 57(4). Urbana, IL: National Council of Teachers of English.

O'Keefe, Timothy. 2001. "Giving Children Voice: Daily Rituals That Support Learning Through Conversations." In *From the Ground Up: Creating a Culture of Inquiry*, eds. Heidi Mills and Amy Donnelly. Portsmouth, NH: Heinemann.

Ray, Katie Wood. 1999. *Wondrous Words*. Urbana, IL: National Council of Teachers of English.

———. 2002. *What You Know by Heart: How to Develop Curriculum for Your Writing Workshop*. Portsmouth, NH: Heinemann.

Short, Kathy. 1997. *Literature as a Way of Knowing*. Portland, ME: Stenhouse.

Short, Kathy, and Carolyn Burke. 1991. *Creating Curriculum: Teachers and Students as a Community of Learners*. Portsmouth, NH: Heinemann.

South Carolina Department of Education. 2005. *South Carolina Science Academic Standards.* Columbia, SC: Author.

Wells, Gordon. 1986. *The Meaning Makers: Children Learning Language and Using Language to Learn.* Portsmouth, NH: Heinemann.

Vygotsky, L. S. 1978. *Mind in Society: The Development of Higher Psychological Processes.* M. Cole, V. John-Steiner, S. Scribner, and E. Sonberman, eds. Cambridge, MA: Harvard University Press.

Children's Books Cited

Asael, Anthony, and Stephanie Rabemiafara. 2011. *Children of the World: How We Live, Learn and Play in Poems, Drawings and Photographs.* New York, NY: Universe Publishing.

Brumbeau, Jeff. 2001. *The Quilt Maker's Gift,* 3rd ed. New York, NY: Scholastic.

Bunting, Eve. 1989. *The Wednesday Surprise.* New York, NY: Clarion Books.

———. 1994. *Sunshine Home.* New York, NY: Clarion Books.

———. 1994. *A Day's Work.* New York, NY: Clarion Books.

———. 1995. *Cheyenne Again.* New York, NY: Clarion Books.

———. 1996. *Terrible Things.* Philadelphia, PA: The Jewish Publication Society.

———. 2006. *One Green Apple.* New York, NY: Clarion Books.

Carson, Ben, and Cecil Murphey. 1996. *Gifted Hands: The Ben Carson Story.* Grand Rapids, MI: Zondervan.

Cole, Joanna. 2004. *The Magic School Bus at the Waterworks.* New York, NY: Scholastic.

Frank, Anne. 1997. *The Diary of a Young Girl: The Definitive Edition.* Otto M. Frank and Mirjam Pressler, eds. New York, NY: Bantam.

Gardiner, John Reynolds. 2010. *Stone Fox.* New York, NY: Harper Collins.

Garland, Sherry. 1997. *The Lotus Seed.* New York, NY: Houghton Mifflin Harcourt.

Gibbons, Gail. 1999. *Penguins!* New York, NY: Holiday House.

———. 2005. *Chicks & Chickens.* New York, NY: Holiday House.

———. 2006. *Owls.* New York, NY: Holiday House.

Giff, Patricia Reilly. 2002. *Nory Ryan's Song.* New York, NY: Yearling.

———. 2006. *A House of Tailors.* New York, NY: Yearling.

Giovanni, Nikki. 2007. *Rosa.* New York, NY: Square Fish.

Henkes, Kevin. 1991. *Chrysanthemum.* New York, NY: Greenwillow Books.

Hesse, Karen. 2009. *Letters from Rifka.* New York, NY: Square Fish.

Juster, Norton. 2005. *The Hello, Goodbye Window.* New York, NY: Hyperion Book CH.

Locker, Thomas. 1995. *Sky Tree: Seeing Science Through Art.* New York, NY: HarperCollins.

Lovell, Patty, and David Catrow. 2001. *Stand Tall, Molly Lou Melon.* New York, NY: G.P. Putnam's Sons.

McCloskey, Robert. 1999. *Make Way for Ducklings.* London: Puffin.

McGill, Alice. 2009. *Molly Bannaky.* Boston, MA: Houghton Mifflin Harcourt.

Mortensen, Greg, and Susan L. Roth. 2009. *Listen to the Wind: The Story of Dr. Greg & Three Cups of Tea.* New York, NY: Penguin.

Myller, Rolf. 1991. *How Big Is a Foot?* New York, NY: Yearling Books.

Pinkney, Andrea Davis. 2010. *Sit-In: How Four Friends Stood Up By Sitting Down.* New York, NY: Little Brown Books for Young Readers.

Polacco, Patricia. 1994. *Pink and Say.* New York, NY: Philomel.

Rosenburg, Liz. 1996. *Grandmother and the Runaway Shadow.* New York, NY: Harcourt Brace & Co.

Sis, Peter, 1996. *Starry Messenger: Galileo Galilei.* New York, NY: Farrar, Straus and Giroux.

Soentpiet, Chris, and Alice McGill. 2009. *Molly Bannaky.* New York, NY: Houghton Mifflin Harcourt.

Woodruff, Elvira. 2000. *The Orphan of Ellis Island: A Time-Travel Adventure.* New York: Scholastic Paperbacks.

Professional Organizations Cited

Rethinking Schools: www.rethinkingschools.org

The Zinn Education Project: http://zinnedproject.org